# INSIDE PASSAGE
## Walking
## Tours

David
GAL

# INSIDE PASSAGE
# Walking
# Tours

*Exploring Major Ports*
*of Call in Southeast Alaska*

J u l i a n n e     C h a s e

SASQUATCH BOOKS
SEATTLE

Printed in Hong Kong.
Distributed in Canada by Raincoast Books Ltd.

02 01 00 99 98     5 4 3 2 1

Cover and interior design, graphics, maps, and composition:
    Rohani Design, Edmonds, Washington
Cover photograph: Copyright Jeff Gnass. West Stock.
Interior photographs: Photographs on pages i, 4, 5, 12, 13 (bot-
    tom), 20, 21, 25 (top), 28, 29 (top), 33, 37, 41, 48, 56 (top), 61
    (bottom), 68, 69, 76, 77, 84 (bottom), 85, 93 (top), 97, 104,
    105, 109, 112, 113, 120, 121, 132, 133, 136, 137, 141, and 144
    copyright ©1998 by Stanton H. Patty. All other photographs by
    author.

Library of Congress Catalog Card Number 97-80682

The information in this book is based in facts available at press
time. Much of it, however, is subject to change, and readers are
advised to check ahead for such things as hours and prices.

Sasquatch Books
615 Second Avenue
Seattle, Washington 98104
(206) 467-4300
books@sasquatchbooks.com
http://www.sasquatchbooks.com
Sasquatch Books publishes high-quality adult nonfiction and
children's books related to the Northwest (Alaska to San
Francisco). For more information about our titles, contact us at
the address above, or view our site on the World Wide Web.

# Contents

# Introduction

The fabled Inside Passage threads its way through Southeast Alaska, a spectacularly beautiful land of islands, rain forests, soaring mist-layered mountains, and abundant wildlife from both land and sea. Some 10,000 years ago massive glaciers of the last ice age sculpted this land, carving the fjords and creating the thousand or so islands that make up the Alexander Archipelago.

Each of the picturesque coastal towns along the Inside Passage has its own flavor: totem poles and fishing boats in Ketchikan; state government and mining activities—both past and present—in Juneau; the Klondike Gold Rush, alive and well in Skagway; and echoes of Russian America in Sitka.

Southeast Alaska also is home to some of the state's first peoples: the Tlingit, Haida, and Tsimshian, whose rich heritage is celebrated in lofty totem poles and beautiful beadwork, basketry, and other artworks throughout the region.

As different as they are from one another, the towns of the Inside Passage share many similarities. The wilderness is only steps away from the concrete of the city streets and the casual outdoor-oriented lifestyle is woven into the fabric of the place. There's a sense of freedom here, reflected in the spirit and independence of the people who call it home. Individuals count here, and they have a "can-do" attitude that ensures that they will indeed make a difference. It's still a place where you can be on a first-name basis with your congress representative or governor.

This book and its walking tours introduce you to the towns of Ketchikan, Juneau, Skagway, and Sitka. You'll find out how they came to be and what it's like to live there, as well as some of the things about them both wonderful and a little weird. All of the walking tours are circular routes; you can start anywhere and return to that point. There's a key to refer to when you want to visit, or return to, a specific spot.

Southeast's climate is cool and often moist. Those who live here both ignore it and give it healthy respect. Plan for the layered look and wear comfortable low-heeled shoes. Sometimes it's warm and sunny, but when it's not, wear an extra sweater, pull on your rain gear and waterproof boots or shoes, and blend in with the locals. Most of all, enjoy your time here, whether it's for a day or a year.

## A WORD ABOUT THE WILDERNESS
Each section of this book includes one or two day hikes that are the most accessible to the town. The following cautionary notes apply to hiking *anywhere* in Southeast Alaska:

- Tell someone where you are going and when you plan to return.
- Carry your own water and snacks, and make sure to pack out your trash.
- Wear your "Southeast sneakers" (rubber boots) or waterproof shoes or boots and stay on the trail.
- Keep an eye out for bears. Most of the islands of Southeast have black bears in residence, but there also are brown bears on the mainland and the "ABC islands": Admiralty, Baranof, and Chichagof Islands (Sitka is on Baranof). If you see a bear, do not approach it or try to feed it. Never get between a mother and her cub. Bears usually prefer to avoid people, so make noise as you go along so you don't surprise one: sing to yourself, talk to others, or jingle "bear bells." National Park and Forest Service offices have more information about bears.

**Population:**   Ketchikan Gateway Borough: 14,000
(15.7% Alaska Natives)
City of Ketchikan: 8,729
52% Men; 48% Women
Visitors: 300,000 + annually

**Geography:**   Ketchikan Gateway Borough: 1,250 sq. mi.
City of Ketchikan: 3.81 sq. mi.
Location: SW coast of Revillagigedo Island,
fronting Tongass Narrows; 235 miles north
to Juneau; 679 miles south to Seattle

**Weather:**   Average summer temperatures: 46–59° F
Average winter temperatures: 29–48° F
Annual precipitation: 162" (13.5'), including
32" of snow

**Primary**
**Industries:**   Fishing (397 residents hold commercial
fishing permits)
Fish-processing facilities
Timber and wood products manufacturing
Tourism (600 cruise ships call annually)
Government (2/3 of the state ferry system
workers live in Ketchikan)

**Facilities**
**and**
**Services:**   A University of Alaska Southeast campus
(500 students); 26 churches; full-service
Ketchikan General Hospital. Newspapers:
*Ketchikan Daily News*, monthlies *Southeast
Log* and *New Alaskan*. Radio: KTKN 930;
KRBD-FM (Rain Bird); public radio: FM
106.7. TV: CFTK (Prince Rupert, B.C.); 27
cable channels.

**Visitor**
**Information:**   Ketchikan Visitors Bureau, 131 Front St.,
(907) 225-6166 or (800) 770-2200. What to
see and do in Ketchikan.
Southeast Alaska Visitor Center, 50 Main St.,
(907) 225-8131. Information on Tongass
National Forest, Misty Fiords National Park,
and other federal agencies.

# Ketchikan

*Ketchikan visitor to small boy on the
dock: "Has it been raining long?"
Small boy: "I don't know. I'm only five
years old."*

"Salmon Capital of the World." It's a big boast, but salmon are Ketchikan's reason for being. Before European explorers came on the scene, generations of Tongass and Cape Fox Tlingits had fish camps on Ketchikan Creek. They gave the place its name: "kitsch-khin," which means "thundering wings of an eagle."

American settlers came to the area in the 1880s, building a salmon saltery at the mouth of Ketchikan Creek. The first cannery opened in 1886; by 1936, Ketchikan was one of the largest exporters of salmon in the world, producing 1.5 million cases of salmon annually.

The need for lumber to build new businesses and homes, as well as packing boxes for the canneries, spawned the Ketchikan Spruce Mills in 1903. Ketchikan became a supply center for area logging, and a pulp mill built at Ward Cove in 1954 helped fuel area growth. (The mill closed in 1997 and the city is seeking new economic development and ventures.)

Today, fishing and tourism power the economy of Ketchikan, which has grown to be Alaska's fourth largest city. In the process, it has earned a couple of additional nicknames: "Alaska's First City," because it's the first city in Alaska that northbound ferries and cruise ships reach, and, more recently, "Totem Town," because of all the totem poles—at least 113—scattered in various locations around the Ketchikan area. The totems, along with colorful Creek Street (a reminder of an earlier, bawdier time), are major draws for visitors.

Even though the body of water in front of town might look like a river, it's not. That saltwater channel is Tongass Narrows. Across the way are Gravina Island and the smaller Pennock Island. Ketchikan itself is on an island: Revillagigedo (ruh-VEE-ah-hey-hey-doe). It was named by Spaniards for the eighteenth-century viceroy of New Spain (Mexico) who supported the Spanish exploration of

Alaska. Instead of trying to pronounce this tongue-twister, just say "Revilla" (ruh-VIL-ah) like the locals do.

Much of downtown Ketchikan was built on pilings. Many of the buildings are original structures and often have trapdoors that were once used by bootleggers. Boardwalks and trestle streets were common in earlier times, and although most have been replaced or paved over, a few can still be seen (Stops #7 and #15 on the walking tour).

*Creek Street is "where fishermen and salmon went upstream to spawn."*

Visitors are fascinated to discover that what may appear to be a street on a map is actually a flight of wooden stairs, often the only access to homes on the steep slopes. Residents sometimes hire helicopters to move heavy furniture in or out of their hillside homes. And, you'd certainly think twice before buying something large and bulky if it had to be hauled up 100 or so stairs.

Downtown Ketchikan is so compact that visitors can go exploring without worrying about losing their way. You can't get far. Only 18.4 miles north and 12.9 miles south, the roads stop. And we're not kidding: The signs literally say "Road Ends." There's also not much crime to speak of, although there was a bank robbery some 20 years ago. Seems a 19-year-old kid with bad judgment robbed First Bank and then raced around the corner—straight into the arms of the police, who were running down Main from the station to answer the bank's silent alarm.

Ketchikan's topography and geology have resulted in some peculiarities. Because of the very thin topsoil, graves at Bayview Cemetery are blasted out of the rock and then filled with dirt. And the town was built literally up the sides of the hills, with some homes at the 100-foot elevation level.

*"Ketchikan is 5 miles long, 7 blocks wide, and 5 inches deep."*

Residents make use of every square inch of their property, often adding on a room here and there as the need arises. And, being an independent lot, they tend not to take no for an answer—even, or maybe especially, from the city fathers. There's a local story about a homeowner who, refused permission to tear down a house and rebuild on his too-small lot, constructed new walls and a roof around the outside of the old house, and then tore it down from the inside out. "You could see the old walls right through the windows of the new one," remembered one local.

*"If you can't see the top of Deer Mountain, it's raining. If you can, it's going to rain."*

Ketchikan is blessed with about 160 inches (more than 13 feet) of precipitation annually—most of it rain. A sunny day is something to celebrate with a spontaneous picnic or fishing trip. However, you might see a few locals walking around looking a little "sun-shocked," with hats pulled low to shade their eyes.

Residents take the rain in stride. They go fishing in the rain. They play sports in the rain. Baseball and soccer games are almost never called on account of rain; they'd never make it through the season otherwise. (Basketball, not surprisingly, is extremely popular throughout Southeast Alaska.)

*Above:* Pulling into "Alaska's First City," Ketchikan, on Tongass Narrows. Behind the cruise ship dock is Thomas Boat Basin. *Left:* This weathered totem pole is part of the nation's largest collection of 19th-century totems, housed at the Totem Heritage Center. *Right:* Measuring Ketchikan's "liquid sunshine"—will it hit the annual average of 13 feet?

LIQUID
SUNSHINE
GAUGE
BUSTED IN 1949
202.55 IN.

EMPTY RAIN CLOUDS GOING
BACK FOR ANOTHER LOAD

WE HAVE THE TALLEST
BAROMETER IN THE WORLD

DEER MTN.          3000 FT.

IF YOU CAN'T SEE THE TOP: IT'S RAINING.
IF YOU CAN SEE THE TOP: IT'S GOING TO RAIN.

WET DATA:
OUR AVERAGE RAINFALL IS 162.27
INCHES A YEAR. OUR LIGHTEST RAIN-
FALL OCCURRED IN 1982 WITH ONLY 8789
INCHES. JANUARY AVERAGE TEMP. IS
38.3, WHILE THE AVERAGE JULY TEMP.
IS A BALMY 55.4.

VISITOR
INFORMATION

DROP IN ON OUR OFFICE:
THAT'S WHAT THE RAIN IS DOING;
IF YOU DON'T, YOU'LL BE ALL WET.

KETCHIKAN
All American City

4TH LARGEST CITY
IN ALASKA

RAINBIRD

KING SALMON CAPITAL
OF THE WORLD

The Tongass National Forest and its array of recreational opportunities is Ketchikan's backyard, but living next to the great outdoors does have its hazards. The best bear-viewing used to be at the dump, but the city has controlled them there, so now the bears have branched out and can be seen occasionally meandering through the streets. Bald eagles have been known to snatch up a small dog or a cat. And a pack of wolves once chased a person up a tree in an outlying area.

*It's easier for women to get a date in Ketchikan: 52% of residents are male, 48% female.*

## FESTIVALS AND OTHER FUN

Among the special events unique to Ketchikan are: the Festival of the North in January, a celebration of musical and theatrical productions, visual and literary arts; Wearable Art Fashion Show and Exhibit in February; Celebration of the Sea in April; King Salmon Derby in May, with $47,000 in prizes for big fish; the June Ketchikan Folk Festival; and the Blueberry Arts Festival in August. Check out the *Ketchikan Daily News* for what's going on when you're there.

## DON'T MISS

Any visitor to Ketchikan shouldn't miss:

- The Totem Heritage Center (Stop #12 on the walking tour), with the nation's largest collection of nineteenth-century totem poles
- The Southeast Alaska Visitor Center (Stop #2), with its excellent exhibits on Native American culture, Southeast Alaska's ecosystems and resources, and the rain forest
- A visit to Creek Street, with its shops and restaurants (Stops #18 and #21)
- A ride on the Westmark Cape Fox funicular (Stop #20) for the spectacular view

# Ketchikan Walking Tour

This walking tour through downtown Ketchikan features historic buildings, totem poles, a fish hatchery, shopping on Creek Street, and scenic viewpoints. The terrain is mostly flat, although a few steep hills are on the route, along with some optional stairclimbs with the reward of a spectacular view at the top. Estimated time: 2-2½ hours—longer if you linger to shop or savor the views. (Note: Numbered walking

tour signs you will encounter refer to the Ketchikan Visitors Bureau's tour; this tour visits all of those stops—and much more—but not necessarily in the same order.)

❶ Start the tour on the cruise ship dock at the blue **Ketchikan Visitors Bureau Information Center**, 131 Front Street, the source of information on local sightseeing and visitor facilities. Outside, look for the Ketchikan Rain Gauge, with tongue-in-cheek information about local weather history. Across the street is Ketchikan's main downtown shopping area. ♿ ✗ PIONEER CAFE

♟ *From the front door of the Visitors Bureau, turn right on Front Street, which curves to become Mill Street.*

❷ To the right is the **Southeast Alaska Visitor Center**, 50 Main Street, one of four Alaska Public Lands Information Centers in the state. You'll find plenty of information about the Tongass National Forest, plus other federal agencies.

Opened in June 1995, the center has excellent dioramas on Native American culture: salmon fishing, wood carving, food preservation and preparation. Other exhibits explore Southeast Alaska's ecosystems and resources.

CITY FLOAT

Tongass Narrows

Cruise Ship Dock

THOMAS BASIN

9.9 miles to Totem Bight

Water St

Main St

Cedar St

Tunnel

Pine St

Miller Ridge Road

Grant St

Bawden St

Grant St

Front St

Main St

Dock St

Edmond St

Park Ave

Harris St

Married Man's Trail

Ketchikan Creek

Mission St

Mill St

Creek St

Park Ave

Stedman St

Woodland Ave

Salmon Rd

Park Ave

Ketchikan Creek

Thomas St

Deermont St

Deermont St

Fair St

To D Moun Trail

Lotus St

Stedman St

2.5 miles to Saxman Village

1
2
3
4
5
6
7
8
9
10
11
12
13
14
15
16
17
18
19
20
21
22
23
24
25
26
27
28

# The Walking Tour

The exhibits are accompanied by sound. In the Native American exhibit, elders tell legends from their history. You'll hear bird calls and waves in the ecosystems exhibit, while the resources exhibit features the actual marine forecast.

There's a theater, trip planning room, and bookstore. Reservations for Forest Service cabins can be made here. Open daily, 8:30 a.m.–4:30 p.m., May 1–Sept. 30; same hours Tues.–Sat., Oct. 1–April 30.

🏧 ♿

🚶 *From the Visitor Center, turn right on Mill Street and go half a block to Bawden Street. Cross over to the park.*

There's a Post Office Substation in the Great Alaska Trading Company across the street. Another option is Mail Boxes, Etc., around the corner at 125 Main Street. ✉

**3** Sit on a bench and admire the flowers at **Whale Park** (named for its shape). The Knox Brothers Clock is Ketchikan's oldest public timepiece. The Chief Kyan totem pole, by master carver Israel Shotridge, was erected in 1993. The crane on top represents Chief Kyan's wife. Just below is the Thunderbird, symbol of his wife's clan. At the bottom is the Bear crest of the chief.

🚶 *From the park, continue right on Bawden to the next corner.*

**4** At Mission and Bawden Streets is **St. John's Episcopal Church and Seamen's Center**. Ketchikan's oldest church, St. John's was built in 1903. Like many older buildings downtown, it was built on fill, and seawater routinely rises in the basement during extremely high tides.

The Seamen's Center, serving those who make their living on and from the sea, was constructed in 1904 as a hospital.

🚶 *From St. John's, turn right up Mission Street, passing along Whale Park, to Dock Street and cross over.*

**5** The **Chief Johnson Totem Pole**, belonging to the Kadjuk House of the Raven Clan of the Tlingit tribe, is a replica carved by Israel Shotridge and raised in 1989. The original, erected in 1901 by Chief Johnson himself, can be seen at the Totem Heritage Center. 📷

🚶 *Proceed left on Dock Street half a block.*

**6** The Centennial Building, 629 Dock Street, houses **Tongass Historical Museum and Public Library**. The library has an extensive Alaskan collection and is a state document repository. The museum has a very good exhibit on Tlingit, Tsimshian, and Haida cultures, developed through consultations with Native elders. Other exhibits show Ketchikan's history as the "Salmon Capital of the World" and the skull of Old Groaner, a bear that made the fatal mistake of stalking people.

Open daily, 8 a.m.–5 p.m., May 15–Sept. 30; 1–5 p.m. on Wed.–Fri. and 1–4 p.m. on Sat.–Sun., Oct. 1–May 14. Admission: May 1–Sept. 30, adults $2; children 12 and under, free. Free admission on Sunday afternoons. No admission charge Oct. 1–May 14. 🚻 ♿

Next to the museum is the "Raven Stealing the Sun" totem pole, raised in 1983, and an overlook to Ketchikan Creek, where you can see spawning salmon during the summer. The giant wooden king salmon sculpture in the creek was created by Jones Yeltatzie, a Haida master carver, in honor of the 1967 centennial of Alaska's purchase from Russia.

*Above:* Magnificent totem poles like this one have earned Ketchikan the nickname "Totem Town." There are at least 113 totem poles in the city and its outlying areas. *Right, top:* One of the 600 cruise ships that visit Ketchikan each year, viewed from the top of the Westmark Cape Fox funicular. *Right:* A net full of smolts (baby salmon) at the Deer Mountain Fish Hatchery on Ketchikan Creek.

🚶 *From the museum, head right on Dock Street half a block, turn right on Bawden Street for one block, then turn right on Park Avenue.*

---

OPTION: *For a shorter tour, featuring the shopping areas of Creek Street and downtown, but skipping the Salmon Ladder, Deer Mountain Fish Hatchery, and the Totem Heritage Center:*

🚶 *Retrace your steps from the museum through the parking lot to the entrance of Creek Street (Stop #21), the funicular (Stop #20), and out to Stedman (Stop #17). Turn right on Stedman Street.*

*Stedman will take you back to the cruise ship pier or to the downtown shopping area.*

---

**❼** Straight ahead as you walk up Bawden Street, you can see the picturesque **Grant Street Trestle**. Now on the National Register of Historic Places, this is Ketchikan's last wood trestle. In the city's early years, all of the sidewalks and streets were built as trestles, so residents could easily negotiate the steep slopes.

Historic buildings you'll pass on Park Avenue include:

- 655 Park Avenue, built in 1908 on a portion of the Venetia Lode gold claim;
- 632 Park Avenue, 1912;
- 639 Park Avenue, early 1920s;
- Ketchikan Apartments at 652 Park Avenue, 1925.

🚶 *Proceed along the righthand side of Park Avenue for 3–5 minutes. Look for a sign on the fence with an arrow pointing the way to the Salmon Ladder. Turn right and follow the boardwalk to a wooden observation deck.*

**❽** The concrete **Salmon Ladder** enables salmon returning from the sea to bypass the falls so they can reach the upper stretches of Ketchikan Creek to spawn. From the deck, watch migrating salmon during the summer. 🚻

🚶 *Retrace your steps to Park Avenue and continue to the right. Cross the street and walk along the creek for about 10 minutes.*

---

OPTION: *For a shorter tour, bypassing the salmon hatchery and Totem Heritage Center and proceeding to the Creek Street shops, look for the sign for the Married Man's Trail on Park Avenue, just as you cross the creek. The trail meanders off to the right for a 2–3 minute walk to Creek Street. Married Man's Trail was so-named because men from the town took this trail through the woods, particularly during Prohibition, to visit the Creek Street bawdy houses to get a drink, play cards, or visit the "sporting women."*

*As a second option, take the upper portion of the trail—up four flights of stairs (65 steps) and then a well-maintained, but unlighted, trail through the woods with peek-a-boo views of the town. It's 10-15 minutes to the Westmark Cape Fox hotel. Then take the funicular down to Creek Street from the hotel lobby.*

---

**❾** Park Street passes through a residential area. There are good views of salmon and fishermen, particularly from the **Harris Street Bridge**. (A note to birdwatchers: Just past Harris Street is Freeman Street, a short dead end. Along the creek across from Freeman is a sandhill crane nesting area. Among the tallest birds in the world, with wingspans of six to seven feet, these birds may be seen throughout Southeast Alaska in the spring and fall.)

🚶 *Park Avenue curves and then crosses a bridge. Just after the bridge, cross the street and head to the right on Salmon Road to the fish hatchery.*

**❿** **Deer Mountain Fish Hatchery** belongs to Ketchikan Tribal Hatchery Corp., a subsidiary of the Ketchikan Indian Corp. Built in 1954, it raises

## GRABBING A BITE

Following are a few suggested dining spots. The number indicates where to look for them as you follow the walking tour.

**PIONEER CAFE,** 124 Front St. (Stop #1). Specialties at the self-described "friendliest place in town" are Alaskan seafood and reindeer sausage. Breakfast, lunch, and dinner. $

**HEEN KAHIDI RESTAURANT,** Westmark Cape Fox Hotel, 800 Venetia Way (Stop # 20). Great views of Tongass Narrows. Specializes in seafood; varied menu from burgers to blintzes. Full bar. Daily breakfast, lunch, dinner. $$$

**FIVE STAR CAFE,** 5 Creek St. (Stop # 21). "Healthy foods with flair," featuring homemade soups, creative salads, espresso drinks, simple dinners. No bar. Breakfast, lunch, dinner. $$

**ANNABELLE'S FAMOUS KEG AND CHOWDER HOUSE,** 326 Front St. (Stop # 28). Features "Alaska hospitality in elegant surroundings" with a 1920s atmosphere. Full bar. Daily lunch and dinner. Breakfast, summers only. $$

and releases some 350,000 baby salmon (smolts) each year.

Interpretive displays depict the life cycle of salmon and visitors can watch hatchery operations. The Tribal Gift Shop supports the hatchery by selling Native arts and crafts, smoked and canned salmon, salmon-skin leather accessories, books and souvenirs.

Open 8:30 a.m. to 4:30 p.m. daily, early May to late September. Guided tours are available; prices are $2 for adults; children 5–12, $1.25; children 4 and under, free. 🚻 ♿

🚶 *Follow the path around the side of the hatchery and along the creek for about a minute to City Park.*

**⓫ City Park** has tree-shaded picnic areas near small ponds originally constructed in the early 1900s as part of the city's first fish hatchery. Volunteers restored the park's fountain in 1989. 🚻 ♿

🚶 *Just inside the park, turn right over a stone footbridge, and walk for 1-2 minutes.*

## STOP TO SHOP

The two main areas for unique boutiques and galleries are downtown across from the cruise ship dock and Creek Street. A few suggested places to stop and shop are:

**SCANLON GALLERY**, 318 Mission St. Works by major Alaskan artists and locals as well as traditional and contemporary Alaska Native artwork.

**SALMON, ETC.**, 322 Mission St. With Ketchikan calling itself the "Salmon Capital of the World," it wouldn't do to leave without some, whether it's smoked, canned, or frozen.

Creek Street has numerous great shops. The Star Building at 5 Creek Street has three in particular that are well worth visiting:

**PARNASSUS** (upstairs). A local bookstore carrying an eclectic assortment of new, old, and Alaska books; classical and jazz music; and distinctive gifts.

**SOHO COHO** (also upstairs). Featuring the droll, wearable artwork of Ketchikan's own Ray Troll (try "Salmon Chanted Evening" on for size).

**ALASKA EAGLE ARTS** (boardwalk level). A fine art gallery featuring Pacific Northwest Native artworks.

**⓬ The Totem Heritage Center**, a National Historic Landmark, houses the nation's largest collection of nineteenth-century totem poles, with some up to 140 years old. The City of Ketchikan built the center in 1976 to preserve and display 33 original totem poles, house posts, and pole fragments from old Tlingit villages on Tongass and Village islands and from the Haida village  of Old Kasaan. All are within 50 miles of Ketchikan and were abandoned around the turn of the century as residents moved away for jobs and schooling.

Exhibits include contemporary Tlingit, Haida, and Tsimshian ceremonial clothing and beadwork and an exhibit of Chilkat weaving. The gift shop sells Native artwork. Information about native plants is posted along a nature trail.

## THE LEGEND OF HOW RAVEN STOLE THE SUN

A traditional Southeast Alaska Native legend tells how Raven brought light to the world. In Ketchikan, visitors will find the story depicted in the totem pole "Raven Stealing the Sun," located next to the museum on Dock Street.

As the legend goes, Raven desired the Sun, Moon, and Stars, which were owned by a powerful chief.

So, Raven changed himself into a spruce needle and fell into a stream. The spruce needle was swallowed by the old chief's daughter as she drank from the stream. She became pregnant and gave birth to a son who was really Raven, the trickster.

The old man loved his grandson and gave him anything he wanted. The child cried and begged for the containers of light and eventually the old chief relented and gave the boxes to the boy.

One by one, Raven opened the boxes, releasing the Sun, the Moon, and the Stars through the lodge's smoke hole. And so it came to pass that Raven brought light to the world.

Open 8 a.m.–5 p.m. daily, May 15–Sept. 30; 1–5 p.m. on Tues.–Fri., Oct. 1–May 14. Admission May 1–Sept. 30 is $3 for adults; children 12 and under free. Free admission on Sunday afternoons. No charge for admission Oct. 1–April 30. 🏳 ♿ (Special exhibits for the blind.)

🚶 *From the front of the Totem Heritage Center, go left to Deermont Street, then turn right down the hill 10-12 minutes to Stedman Street and turn right.*

🔟🟢 As you round the corner, across Stedman Street, you'll see the **"Return of the Eagle"** mural on the University of Alaska Southeast's Robertson Building. The 70 × 120-foot mural, commissioned by the Ketchikan Indian Corporation and local arts groups in 1978, was painted by artist Don Barrie and 25

## CREEK STREET'S COLORFUL LEGACY

Colorful Creek Street (Stops #18 and #21) is "where fishermen and salmon went upstream to spawn."

A plank street built on pilings over Ketchikan Creek, the street began its notorious era as Ketchikan's official red light district in 1903, when the City Council banished all the bawdy houses south of Ketchikan Creek to Creek Street and south Stedman.

During its heyday, more than 30 houses on Creek Street were operated by "sporting women," as they preferred to call themselves. Because a Territorial law defined a house of prostitution as a place inhabited by more than two "female boarders" (a euphemism for prostitutes), most Creek Street houses were occupied by only one or two women, who went by such fanciful names as Frenchy, Black Mary, and Dirty Neck Maxine.

Before, during, and after Prohibition, these sporting gals also ran speakeasies, supplied by bootleggers operating from the Canadian port of Prince Rupert, British Columbia, a convenient 90 miles south. Liquor was hoisted through trapdoors from the bootleggers' boats at high tide. The houses were shut down in 1953 after a grand jury investigation of several scandals, two of which involved the chief of police and a police captain (both were indicted and convicted).

The most famous of the Creek Street residents was Dolly Arthur, the "stage name" of one Thelma Copeland. Dolly's House is now a museum (Stop #19). Most of the other houses along picturesque Creek Street are now shops or restaurants; a few remain private residences.

Native youths, who illustrated traditional stories within a shield motif.

🚶 *Continue to the right on Stedman Street for 4-5 minutes.*

**14** Next stop is **Shotridge Studios Cultural Center and Museum**, 407 Stedman Street. Here you may meet Israel Shotridge, the master carver who created the Chief Kyan and Chief Johnson totem poles. Watch him work on a totem pole or see other artists demonstrating traditional crafts. There's also a museum and gift shop.

🚶 *Cross Stedman Street and turn left on Thomas Street.*

*Above:* A costumed "sporting woman" greets visitors to Dolly's House, one of Creek Street's more [in]famous residences. *Right, top:* Fishing boats and pleasure craft moored in Thomas Boat Basin. *Right:* Ketchikan's former red light district, Creek Street, "where fishermen and salmon went upstream to spawn."

**15** Thomas Street, one of the few remaining wooden streets in Ketchikan, originally provided access to

the former New England Fish Company cannery. Entering the street, you'll pass 148 Thomas Street, built in 1912 and part of the **Thomas Street Historic District**.

Near the end of the street, which narrows to sidewalk width, look over the side and you'll see grids of heavy timbers used to support boats so their hulls can be painted or repaired at low tide.

A variety of maritime- and commercial fishing-related businesses are in the area, including the Potlatch Bar, 126 Thomas Street, known as "the fishermen's bar." The end of the boardwalk affords good views of the fishing fleet, the cruise ship dock, and the city.

🚶 *Retrace your steps on Thomas Street and turn left to the Thomas Street Viewing Platform.*

**16** The **Thomas Street Viewing Platform** is an excellent place to photograph the fishing boats and pleasure craft in Thomas Basin. A kiosk has a display about the fishing industry and its role in Ketchikan's history and economy. Wood benches and tables make lingering a pleasure.

🚶 *Continue along the viewing platform and boardwalk back to Stedman Street, turn left, and walk to the bridge.*

**17** From the **Stedman Street Bridge**, spanning the mouth of Ketchikan Creek, you can watch salmon heading upstream to spawn, and fishermen young and old trying to catch them. Ketchikan Creek produces four of the five species of salmon, including king (chinook) from June to mid-August; coho (silver) from September through October; and pink (humpy) and chum (dog) from mid-July through August. From

> ### THE LOWDOWN ON
> ### KETCHIKAN'S AIRPORT
>
> Ketchikan has had an airport only since 1973. It had to be built across Tongass Narrows on Gravina Island—a short ferry ride away—because there was no flat land on Revillagigedo Island. It may be the only airport in the world that has its control tower situated lower than the runway—the runway is raised, so just the top of the tower sticks up past the runway level. Before the airport opened, locals had to board the jets at the World War II-era, military-built airfield on Annette Island, 17 miles south of Ketchikan. They flew over to Annette via war-surplus PBYs (Catalinas), Grumman Goose, and an assortment of other amphibious and pontoon-equipped aircraft.

late fall through May, the big fish in the creek are steelhead trout.

🚶 *Cross Stedman to the entrance of Creek Street and the viewing platform.*

⓲ **Creek Street** is Ketchikan's former red light district. During its heyday, the board street had more than thirty houses of ill repute.

Today, this is a major shopping area, with most of the houses converted to shops or restaurants, although a few remain private residences. Creek Street is a Historic District; notable buildings include:

- #28 Creek Street, which was built in 1899;
- #24 Creek Street, c.1906, now a museum;
- and #5 Creek Street, the Star Building, built in 1898 (the star inlaid in the hardwood floor is a legacy of the building's earlier life as a dance hall).

🚶 *Continue along Creek Street a minute or less to #24, a light green house with red trim.*

*Left:* Begonias bloom cheerfully in window boxes along Creek Street's boardwalk. *Above, top:* Kayakers paddle the calm waters of Ketchikan Creek, where bootleggers once delivered their wares to speakeasies through trapdoors at high tide. *Above:* Boardwalks edge the creek, while former brothels—now shops or residences--cling to the hillside along picturesque Creek Street.

**19** #24 Creek Street, built around 1906, is **Dolly's House**. Dolly Arthur was Ketchikan's most famous

"sporting woman." The home where she lived from 1919 until 1973 is now a private museum. Self-guided tours are available when cruise ships are in port; there is an admission charge.

Visitors will see Dolly's own furniture and other belongings throughout the house, a secret cupboard for bootleg liquor, an interesting "facility" for gentlemen visitors, and more. Recordings in several rooms narrate Dolly's story.

🚶 *Turn right and continue along Creek Street's winding boardwalk for 5 minutes (or more, depending on how much shopping you do). Toward the other end of Creek Street is the Cape Fox Hotel's funicular.*

**20** Near the entrance to the funicular, look around the corner to the left to see a tunnel approximately 10 feet deep in the rock face. This is a Venetia Lode mine "adit" (shaft) dug by miners in the 1890s to fulfill the requirement that they do some work

every year to "prove up" their claim even though nothing much ever came of the mine work.

The **Cape Fox funicular**, a tram that operates like an elevator, runs 130 feet up the side of Boston Smith Hill to the lobby of the Westmark Cape Fox Hotel. (Sometimes there is a small charge to ride the funicular, but usually it is free. It shuts down at midnight.)

The hotel, built and owned by the Cape Fox Indian Corporation, opened in 1990. From the top, you'll have a panoramic view of Tongass Narrows and the city below. Centerpiece of the lobby is the large cedar "Sun Raven" screen, by internationally renowned master carver Nathan Jackson. Out the front entrance, you'll see a collection of six 10-foot totem poles by another acclaimed carver, Lee Wallace. "The Council of Clans" represents Tlingit clan figures of Saxman Village. 📷 ✕ HEEN KAHIDI RESTAURANT

Across the parking lot is the Ted Ferry Civic Center. ♿ ♿

**🚶 *Retrace your steps back through the Cape Fox lobby to the funicular and return to Creek Street. Follow the boardwalk toward the right to the footbridge.***

**㉑** The **footbridge across Ketchikan Creek** is a good spot to photograph Creek Street and to watch migrating salmon. A kiosk on the other side has historical information about Creek Street. 📷 ✕ FIVE STAR CAFE

**🚶 *Continue through the parking lot to Dock Street. Proceed to the right for about a block and a half to the corner of Dock and Edmond Streets and turn right.***

**㉒** The Ketchikan Daily News building on the corner was built in 1925 as a U.S. Post Office. Take a moment to read the plaque on the side of the newspaper building before continuing to **Edmond Street**, named for Agnes Edmond, an Episcopal missionary who arrived in 1898—the third white woman, and first single one, to live in Ketchikan.

You'll notice right away that Edmond Street isn't. A street, that is. Adapting to the terrain in true Ketchikan style, Edmond Street is a flight of 126 stairs, with nine landings on which to catch your breath. It's worth the climb. From the top, there's a great view of downtown Ketchikan, Deer Mountain, and Tongass Narrows. 📷

**🚶 *Retrace your steps to Dock Street and turn right for a block to Main Street, then turn right up the hill.***

Downtown Ketchikan's two ATMs are at National Bank of Alaska and First Bank, on opposite corners at the intersection of Dock and Main Streets. 🏧

*Left, top:* The clan house at Saxman Village. *Left:* One of the many dramatic totem pole carvings that can be seen throughout the Ketchikan area. *Above, top:* Tumble-down buildings near George Inlet Cannery, north of Ketchikan. *Above:* View of downtown and Tongass Narrows from the Edmond Street stairs.

## WHAT TIME IS HIGH TIDE?

Ketchikan's elevation is sea level, although some of its neighborhoods rise to an ear-popping 100 feet.

If you've arrived by ship in the morning and come back in the afternoon, you will probably find either that the gangway enters the ship on a different deck or the gangway itself slopes at a greater or lesser degree than it did when you left. You're not imagining things. This is because (you may have noticed this) the ship floats. And, it floats up and down with the fluctuation of Ketchikan's 20 foot tides.

Tides are the alternate rise and fall of the earth's oceans, caused by the gravitational pull of the moon and the sun. Tides occur twice during each lunar day, which is 24 hours and 51 minutes, and which is why the tide is never high or low at the same time during our standard 24-hour day.

So, it's true that "time and tide wait for no man," but if you have a tide book (available at many locations, including drug and sporting goods stores), you can impress your friends by telling them when they can see the next high (or low) tide.

**㉓** On the way up the **Main Street hill**, you'll cross Grant Street, named for turn-of-the-century resident O.W. "Six-Shooter" Grant, who was always armed and rumored to sleep with his pistols. Across Grant from the police station, the large concrete edifice is the State Office Building.

🚶 *At Grant, cross the street to continue up the hill.*

As you pass by First Methodist Church, notice that the parking stalls are marked with—what else?—Roman numerals.

🚶 *Continue up Main Street to the totem pole at the intersection of Main and Pine Streets.*

**㉔** At the foot of the Main Street stairs is the **Chief Kyan Totem**, commissioned by Tlingit Chief George Kyan. Feel lucky? Local lore says if you touch this totem pole, you'll have money in your hands within 24 hours.

Overlooking the totem pole is the turreted **Monrean House**. On the National Register of Historic Places, the Queen Anne-style home was constructed in 1904 for H.Z. Burkhart, builder of Ketchikan's first sawmill.

🚶 *Continue left on Pine Street for one block and turn right onto the Front Street Overlook.*

---

OPTION: *The Main Street Stairs offer another opportunity to take a climb—120 steps to the top. There are good views of Tongass Narrows and downtown on the way up, but the view from the top is obscured by trees.* 📷

---

**25** A boardwalk extension of the street, the **Front Street Overlook** clings to the side of the hill, affording spectacular views and photo opportunities of Tongass Narrows, the busy waterfront, and Gravina and Pennock Islands. 📷

Most of the large homes in this Nob Hill area around Pine and Front Streets were built in the early 1900s for local merchants.

🚶 *Retrace your steps back to Pine and go straight ahead, then down the 116 steps of the Front Street Stairs. At the bottom, turn to the right through the tunnel (the street becomes Water Street on the other side of the tunnel).* 📷

**26** Drilling of the **Ketchikan Tunnel** through Nob Hill was completed in 1954. Prior to that, traffic went around the side of the hill on one-lane Water Street, alternating directions for a few minutes at a time. When a pulp mill was built at nearby Ward Cove, fueling the town's growth, another roadway was needed to accommodate the traffic. Since many of the city fathers lived atop Nob Hill and opposed blasting it to smithereens, the tunnel was the solution.

The 273-foot-long Ketchikan Tunnel is listed in the *Guinness Book of World Records* as the only one anywhere that you can drive over, around, and through.

🚶 *At the other end of the tunnel, cross Water Street and proceed half a block.*

**㉗** From **Harborview Park**, overlooking the City Float, you can see fishing boats, float planes, and

marine traffic on Tongass Narrows. Decorated with hanging flower baskets in the summer, the park also has lots of wooden benches and picnic tables. On the way to the park, get an espresso or a cold drink to enjoy as you sit and watch the waterfront action.

🚶 *Turn right and head back on Water Street, this time around the outside of Nob Hill.*

**㉘** Rounding the hill, you'll come to **Eagle Park**. Its centerpiece is the "Thundering Wings" totem, carved by internationally renowned Tlingit master carver Nathan Jackson.

Across the street, side by side, are the Ketchikan Gateway Borough offices and Ketchikan City Hall, should you get the urge to conduct municipal business. ✗ ANNABELLE'S FAMOUS KEG AND CHOWDER HOUSE

🚶 *Cross the street and continue right on Front Street.*

Between the drugstore and the barber shop, there's a white door. If it's open, as it often is during the summer, peek in to see two trap doors in the floor—reminders of Ketchikan's old bootlegging days.

🚶 *Continue another 2-3 minutes back to the cruise ship dock and the end of the walking tour.*

# Getting Out of Town

## TAKE A HIKE: DEER MOUNTAIN TRAIL

For quick trip to the great outdoors, 3.1-mile Deer Mountain Trail is the closest to downtown Ketchikan. Deer Mountain is a 3,001-foot "horn," a pointy peak left after the glaciers receded 10,000 to 15,000 years ago.

The trailhead is at the intersection of Deermont and Fair Streets. To get there from downtown, head south on Stedman Street and turn left on Deermont. Walk up the hill for 15 to 20 minutes, to Fair Street, and then follow the signs to the trail. (You can also take a taxi to the trailhead.)

The well-used trail winds up the mountain through rain forest that quickly begins thinning out. It's relatively steep in places, so allow enough time (two to three hours) for a leisurely pace and to enjoy the views along the way. The peak affords panoramic views of Ketchikan, Tongass Narrows, and the neighboring islands. (Refer to page vii for general advice about hiking in Southeast Alaska.)

## PLAY MISTY (FIORDS) FOR ME

Ketchikaners enjoy one of the biggest backyards in the world, the 16.9-million-acre Tongass National Forest.

All of Revillagigedo Island is in the national forest, which is the largest in the nation. Nearby (35 minutes by float plane) is dramatic 2.3-million-acre Misty Fiords National Monument, a rugged and scenic wilderness punctuated by vertical rock faces, plunging waterfalls, and narrow waterways, and accessible only by boat or float plane. Visitors can see ancient petroglyphs; mountain goats, deer, or bear; and the 234-foot-tall volcanic core called New Eddystone Rock in East Behm Canal.

For an up-close wilderness experience, rent a Forest Service cabin for the bargain rate of $25 a night. You'll get a fly-in or hike-in cabin equipped with a stove for heating and cooking, an outhouse, and wooden bunks (bring your own food, water, sleeping bags). Reserve a cabin at the U.S. Forest Service office in the Southeast Alaska Visitor Center, at 50 Main Street (Stop #2) or call (907) 228-6214.

For a quicker, but equally sensational visit to Misty Fiords, take a flightseeing excursion, which can be booked on board cruise ships or by calling Taquan Air, (907) 225-880, or Ketchikan Air, (907) 225-9888. The Ketchikan Visitors Bureau on the downtown dock has information about other tours.

## TOTEM TOWN: SAXMAN NATIVE VILLAGE

The Ketchikan area has the largest Native American population of any in the state; nearly 16 percent of the population is Tsimshian, Tlingit, or Haida, and their cultures flourish here. Saxman Native Village, 2.5 miles south of Ketchikan, features one of the world's largest collection of totem poles (26 poles, some over 100 years old), a petroglyph rock, a traditional clan house, a production of Tlingit songs and dances by the Cape Fox Dancers, and master carvers and apprentices at work in the carving center. Local arts and crafts are available at the Village Store. Admission to the totem park and store is free.

Reach Saxman via a walking path along the South Tongass Highway (follow Stedman Street out of town and keep going); by taxi (city bus doesn't run to Saxman); or on a tour available on board cruise ships or locally from Cape Fox Tours (P.O. Box 8558, Ketchikan, AK 99901; call (907) 225-5163 for tour information). The Village Store also sells tour tickets.

## TOTEM BIGHT STATE HISTORICAL PARK

Located 9.9 miles north of Ketchikan on North Tongass Highway, Totem Bight State Historical Park is a re-created Native village, situated in the rain forest on a point overlooking Tongass Narrows. The park, on the National Register of Historic Places, was created in the 1930s as a Civilian Conservation Corps project under which skilled local carvers salvaged and re-created totem poles from abandoned villages that were in danger of destruction by the elements.

The park, reached by a short wooded path from a parking lot on the highway, has a replica of a clan house and 14 totems. Free admission; park open dawn to dusk, year-round; clan house open 8 a.m.–8 p.m., Monday–Friday, mid-May to mid-September; 9 a.m.–3 p.m., mid-September to mid-May.

Totem Bight is easily accessible by car or taxi (city bus does not run this far). It is also included in tours available on board cruise ships or locally from several companies, including Gray Line of Alaska, (907) 225-5930.

**Juneau at a Glance**

| | |
|---|---|
| **Population:** | City and Borough of Juneau: 30,209 (12.9% Alaska Natives); 50.7% Men; 49.3% Women; Visitors: 600,000 annually |
| **Geography:** | City and Borough of Juneau: 2,593.6 sq. mi. Location: Mainland of Southeast Alaska panhandle, fronting Gastineau Channel; 600 air miles northwest to Anchorage, 900 air miles southeast to Seattle |
| **Weather:** | Average summer temperatures: 44–65° F Average winter temperatures: 25–35° F Annual precipitation: 92" downtown, 54" just 10 miles north at the airport Average annual snowfall: 101" Tides: Range from 20.2 feet to -4.8 feet Solstices: Summer (June 21): 18 hours, 18 minutes of daylight. Winter (Dec. 21): 6 hours, 21 minutes of daylight. |
| **Primary Industries:** | Government (45% of all jobs). Tourism (460+ cruise ship calls annually). Support services for logging and fishing. Three fish hatcheries and fish processing facilities. Mining |
| **Facilities and Services:** | A University of Alaska Southeast campus; 40 churches; Bartlett Memorial Hospital. Newspapers: *Daily Juneau Empire;* weeklies: *The Paper, Capital City Weekly.* Radio: KINY-AM 800; KJNO-AM 630; KTOO-FM 104.3 (Alaska Public Radio); KTKU-FM 105.1; KSUP-FM 106. TV: KJUD Channel 8; JATV (cable); KTOO (public television). |
| **Visitor Information:** | Juneau Convention & Visitors Bureau, 134 3rd St., (907) 586-2201 or 2284. What to see and do in Juneau. Also kiosk in Marine Park and the cruise ship terminal. U.S. Forest Service Information Center, Centennial Hall, 101 Egan Driven, (907) 586-8751. Tongass National Forest, Forest Service cabins, hikes. |

# Juneau

*"It's pretty common to see the governor walking to work."*

—Juneau resident

J uneau, the first town founded in Alaska after the United States purchased the territory from Russia in 1867, was created by gold miners—and gold diggers seeking to strike it rich off the miners.

This was a fishing area used by Tlingits since time immemorial. In 1879, John Muir, the famous naturalist, visited Gastineau Channel. Muir's observations of mineralization on Mount Roberts drew great interest in Sitka, where German engineer George E. Pilz was developing a mine.

Pilz offered 100 Hudson's Bay blankets and work at the mine to any Tlingit tribe that could bring him promising ore samples. Chief Kowee of the Auk Tribe, which had villages near present-day Juneau, produced several such samples. Pilz grubstaked two prospectors, Joe Juneau and Richard T. Harris, and sent them off to Gastineau Channel. They returned empty-handed, but Pilz dispatched them again in October 1880, this time escorted by Chief Kowee. Kowee took the pair up Gold Creek to Silver Bow Basin—and the mother lode. The boom was on.

With the discovery of gold came a 160-acre townsite—initially named Harrisburgh, but renamed Juneau in 1882.

Numerous mines sprang up on both sides of the channel, including the huge Alaska-Juneau mine on the side of Mount Roberts, built in 1916. The A-J became the largest operation of its kind, producing at its peak 13,000 tons of ore a day. Total production was more than 3.5 million ounces of gold, valued at over $80 million. By the 1930s, mining had declined, and the A-J closed in 1944.

Juneau's economy did not rely solely on gold mining, however. Fishing, canneries, transportation and trading services, and a sawmill all con-
tributed to its growth. Government operations became more important with statehood in 1959 and today 45 percent of Juneau's populace hold government jobs.

Situated below 3,576-foot Mount Juneau and 3,819-foot Mount Roberts, Juneau is undoubtedly one of the prettiest capital cities in the United States. The body of water in front of downtown is Gastineau Channel, where you sometimes can see whales, along with sea kayakers, fishing boats, and other maritime traffic. Across the channel is Douglas Island, part of the Alexander Archipelago, which protects the waterways of the Inside Passage from the Pacific Ocean.

*Juneau's cost of living is about 24 percent higher than Seattle's.*

With a population just topping 30,000, Alaska's third largest city is a place of contrasts. There's the hustle-bustle and deal-making self-importance of "The Session," when the Legislature comes to town. But there's also an informality that leaves room for a hand-printed "Closed for family fishing day" sign to be posted on a shop door on a sunny Sunday at the end of the tourist season. "It's pretty common to see the governor walking to work," noted a local. And when the big Fred Meyer grocery/department store opened, the whole town attended the festivities.

Because of fog and clouds, airplanes aren't always able to land in Juneau, so "overheading" is a common occurrence. Overheading can entail bouncing between Seattle and Anchorage for a day or more, without being able to land in Juneau. People have been known to overhead for three days, or get off the plane in Sitka and take the ferry to Juneau.

Although it's on the mainland, you can't drive anywhere from Juneau. The city has 160 miles of roadways, but the three main routes all end in the forest. Driving "out the road" is popular on sunny days or when cabin fever strikes. The options are driving 5.5 miles south on Thane Road, 40 miles north on the Glacier Highway, or 13 miles on the North Douglas Highway, across the channel.

*On clear nights look for the aurora borealis above Mt. Juneau.*

With the 17-million-acre Tongass National Forest at its back door, Juneau does not lack for outdoor-related recreational opportunities, from the active—hiking, biking, skiing, golf, kayaking, sailing, camping—to the more relaxed, such as the fireside chats at the Mendenhall Glacier Visitor Center in the wintertime. Juneau is also known for its arts and entertainment scene. Numerous art galleries feature the work of local artists. The city has a professional theater company—Perseverance Theatre—as well as community theater, opera, and symphony.

*Juneau has 1,900 registered boats, 1 for every 14 residents.*

Community involvement and pride are evident in the downtown area, where flowers and a beautification program have spruced it up over the past decade. The city offers a charming blend of old and new, big and small.

### FESTIVALS AND OTHER FUN

Special events unique to Juneau include: the Alaska Folk Festival in early April, a week-long celebration featuring folk music and dance, concerts, workshops, and jam sessions; Juneau Jazz and Classics in May, a 10-day festival featuring top jazz and classical musicians from around the world; the Golden North Salmon Derby in August, with prizes for

*Above:* Colorful flowers brighten Juneau's Seawalk; in the background is the Naa Kahidi Theater and Mount Roberts. *Right:* "Hard Rock Miner" sculpture on the waterfront is dedicated to Juneau's miners. *Right, top:* Mendenhall Glacier viewed from North Douglas Island. *Right, bottom:* Lively South Franklin Street shopping and historic district.

catching big fish, including $25,000 for one specially tagged salmon; December's Gallery Walk, a holiday celebration with gallery receptions featuring artists and their work. Look in the *Juneau Empire* or call (907) 586-JUNO to find out what's going on while you're there.

## DON'T MISS
Juneau attractions that you shouldn't miss:

- The Alaska State Museum (Stop # 23 on the walking tour), with an excellent collection of Alaskana, Native cultures, Russian history, and more
- The view from the terrace of the State Office Building (Stop #21)
- Alaska's State Capitol (Stop #14), which offers free, guided tours in the summer
- A visit to Juneau's drive-in glacier, Mendenhall, an awe-inspiring river of ice 3,000 years old, 12 miles long, 1½ miles wide, and a hundred feet deep
- A ride on the Mount Roberts Tramway, 2,000 feet above Juneau (Stop #4)

## GRABBING A BITE
The following are a few suggested dining spots. The number indicates where to look for them along the walking tour.

- Giorgio at the Pier, 544 S. Franklin St. (Stop #4) "Fresh Alaska seafood prepared with Italian flair," plus pizza and pasta in one of Juneau's snazziest restaurants. The prix fixe meal is a very good value. Deck dining in the summer. Full bar. Lunch and dinner. $$$
- City Cafe, 439 S. Franklin St. (Stop #5) Meet the locals at this friendly Juneau institution (since 1912). Featuring American, Chinese and Filipino cuisine. Espresso, beer, wine. Breakfast, lunch, dinner. $
- Silverbow Inn and Restaurant, 120 Second St. (Stop #11) Imaginative meals featuring local seafood in an elegant, historic building. The site of a bakery since 1890, with turn-of-the-century brick ovens still in use. Beer; extensive wine list. Dinner. $$–$$$
- Olivia's Mexican Restaurant, downstairs at 222 Seward St. (Between Stops #11 and #12) Delicious, genuine

Mexican specialties such as chile verde and posole. Very popular. Lunch and dinner. $

- Fiddlehead Restaurant, 429 W. Willoughby Ave. (Between Stops #22 and #23) Close to the State Museum. A renowned local (nay, regional) favorite serving creative, "healthy" foods: homemade soups, pastas, local seafood, home-baked breads, sinful desserts. Live jazz and folk music in the more upscale Fireweed Room upstairs. Full bar. Breakfast, lunch, dinner. $–$$$.

## STOP TO SHOP

Juneau's downtown abounds in boutiques, galleries, and gift shops, most notably along Franklin, Front, and Seward Streets. Prices range from inexpensive to stratospheric. A few suggestions are:

- Decker Gallery, 233 S. Franklin St. One of the few places in Alaska, or anywhere else, to find the works of Rie Munoz, a longtime Juneau artist who paints cheerful scenes of everyday Alaskan life.
- Taku Smokeries, 230 S. Franklin St. Locally caught and smoked salmon; fresh frozen halibut and salmon; and "fishellaneous" gifts.
- Big City Books, 100 N. Franklin St., and Hearthside Books, corner of Front and Franklin Streets; both have extensive selections of Alaska books.
- Mt. Juneau Trading Post, 151 S. Franklin St. It's been here forever (well, almost). Features Northwest Coast art: totems, masks, argillite stone carvings. Ivory, jade, amber jewelry. Also Eskimo crafts, such as baskets, dolls, ivory carvings.
- Annie Kaill's Fine Craft Gallery, 244 Front St. Hand-painted clothing, pottery, prints, and other creative, colorful gifts.

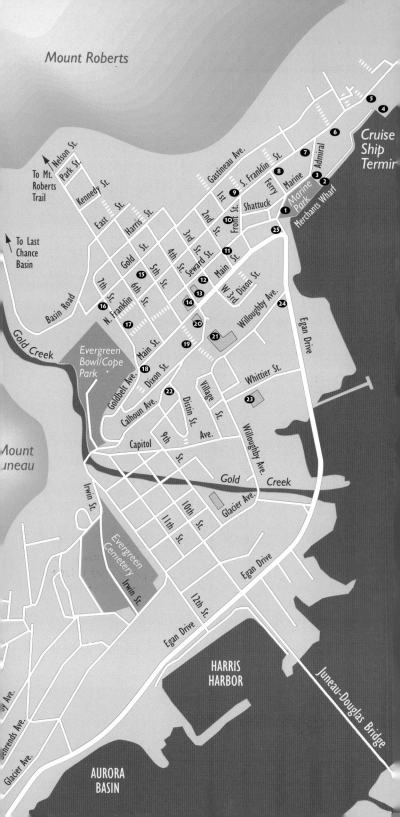

# The Walking Tour

# Juneau Walking Tour

This walking tour through Alaska's capital city covers mostly flat terrain, with a few hills, some of them steep. It takes you through Juneau's main downtown shopping area and to the State Capitol and Governor's Mansion, St. Nicholas Russian Orthodox Church, the city museum, and the State Museum, with some great views and many historic buildings along the way. Estimated time is 2 to 2½ hours—or more, depending on stops along the way.

**1** Begin at **Marine Park** on the central waterfront. Across Marine Way is the City and Borough of

Juneau building (155 S. Seward Street), with a mural that depicts the Tlingit creation myth. 🏛

Nearby is an information kiosk and Ed Way's large bronze sculpture **"Hard Rock Miner,"** dedicated to Juneau's gold miners. Watch the world go by from a large sheltered pavilion; free concerts on Fridays, 7:00–8:30 p.m., June through mid-August.

🚶 *From the sculpture, head toward the channel and turn left on the boardwalk.*

**2** **Juneau's Seawalk** affords great views: the Alaska-Juneau Mine ruins on the side of Mount Roberts; cruise ships, floatplanes, and fishing boats in Gastineau Channel. Barrels of flowers brighten the way spring through fall. 📷

🚶 *Proceed for 2 to 3 minutes along the Seawalk to the first large building on the left.*

❸ The **Juneau Library** was built in 1988–89 atop a four-story parking garage, a design deemed so noteworthy it made the cover of *Architectural Digest*.

An elevator provides easy access to the fifth floor and its panoramic views. A stained glass window depicts salmon changing into figures from Tlingit mythology.

Outside on the channel side, there's a mural of a turn-of-the-century steamship. On the dock near the corner of the library is a bronze sculpture of **Patsy Ann**, an English bull terrier that once greeted all arriving steamships.

🚶 *Continue along the Seawalk for 5 minutes. At the end, turn left and cross the bridge.*

❹ The **Cruise Ship Terminal** houses an information center—another place to find out what to see and do in Juneau. Public telephones. 📞
Giorgio at the Pier (544 S. Franklin Street) is to the south, across the parking lot from the Cruise Ship Terminal. ✕ GIORGIO AT THE PIER

Also just to the south is the lower terminal for the **Mount Roberts Tramway**.

🚶 *From the information center, go straight ahead to South Franklin Street and turn left.*

❺ Juneau's **main shopping area**—loaded with boutiques and galleries—is along South Franklin Street, along with a portion of the **Downtown Historic District**, with many turn-of-the century buildings. The street's namesake is Howard Franklin, who led the miners' committee that laid out the original townsite. The street runs along the original waterfront; the area on the water side has been filled in with rock "tailings" from the A-J Mine.

Sidewalks here are grooved to resemble old-time boardwalks; some "sidewalks" are steep stairways up the mountainside.

*Left:* Mt. Roberts Tramway ascends 2,000 feet above the Juneau waterfront. *Top:* Cruise ships dock in Juneau from May through September. *Bottom:* Ornate, Queen Anne-style Valentine Building at Front and Seward.

Across from the Cruise Ship Terminal is the **Inn at the Waterfront** (455 S. Franklin Street). Built in 1914 as the Scandinavian Rooms, the former brothel was renovated in 1987, winning a city commendation for historic renovation. This neighborhood was once known as "The Line," where "ladies of the evening" and speakeasies operated openly. Juneau's former red light district, Alaska's largest and longest-running, operated from 1881 to 1958. A few doors to the left is the City Cafe (439 S. Franklin Street). ✗ CITY CAFE

🚶 *Proceed up South Franklin Street for 2 to 3 minutes.*

**❻** On the lefthand side is **Sealaska Cultural Arts Park**. Daily performances featuring Tlingit, Haida, and Tsimshian Native storytelling are scheduled from June through September at the **Naa Kahidi Theater**, a replica of a clan house (call (907)586-3571 for times and ticket information). Drop in at the **Alaska Native Arts Market** to watch Native artists at work or purchase arts and crafts.

🚶 *Continue on South Franklin Street to Admiral Way.*

**❼** Across Admiral Way near the library is the current location of the famous **Red Dog Saloon** (it's had at least two previous addresses in the vicinity), complete with swinging door, sawdust floors, and assorted oddities such as Wyatt Earp's pistol. The Juneau Police Department is conveniently located next door.

🚶 *Cross Admiral Way and proceed along the lefthand side of Franklin Street about 10 minutes (or more if you stop to shop) to Front Street.*

**❽** Among the **historic buildings** along Franklin Street between Admiral Way and Front Street are:

- The Senate Building (175 S. Franklin Street), built in 1898 and now a shopping mall.
- The Alaska Steam Laundry Building (174 S. Franklin Street), constructed in 1901 and on the National Register of Historic Places. It's also a shopping mall. Wander its hallways to see a collection of photographs dating back to the 1880s.
- The Alaskan Hotel (167 S. Franklin Street), built in 1913 and also on the National Register. It is Juneau's oldest continuously operating hotel. Note the ornate tin ceiling if you drop in; its bar is a favorite local watering hole and a good place to try an Alaskan Amber Ale or Pale Ale from Juneau's own microbrewery.

🚶 *Continue to the clock at Franklin and Front Streets.*

---

OPTION:

🚶 *From the clock, walk a block and a half up Franklin to the Westmark Baranof Hotel.*

The **Westmark Baranof Hotel** (105 Franklin Street) is named for Lord Alexander Baranov, governor of Russian America (who probably never visited the Juneau area). Built in 1938–39, the 10-story, Art Moderne-style hotel cost $550,000 to build—hard to come by during the Depression—and was Alaska's most modern hotel. Seriously damaged by fire in 1984, the hotel has been restored to its original decor. Its public rooms feature a collection of paintings by famous Alaskan masters, including Sydney M. Laurence, Eustace Paul Ziegler, and Don Clever. Hobnob in the Bubble Room with Alaska politicians during the Legislative session, which begins in January.

**👫 Retrace your steps back downhill to Front Street, turn right at the clock.**

**❾** Across Franklin Street from the clock is **Gunkadeit Park**, which takes its name from a mythological Tlingit lake monster—depicted on a plaque in the park—who brings good fortune to those who see him.

**👫 From the clock, continue along Front Street one block to Seward Street.**

**❿** **Front Street** traces Juneau's former high-tide line; buildings on the left-hand side originally were built on pilings over the beach.

Among Front Street's historic buildings are:

- The Imperial Bar (241 Front Street), built in 1891 and the oldest saloon in Alaska to operate continuously at the same location. A brothel was once located upstairs; occasionally, the madam would direct an unwelcome customer to a certain door in the side of the building—on pilings at the time—and he'd step out right into the channel.
- Now housing retail shops, 205 Front Street is one of Juneau's oldest buildings, built c.1884 as a hardware store. The hardware store across the alley (225 Front Street) has operated since about 1895.
- Lawyer Jack Hellenthal built his namesake building at 220 Front Street in 1916.
- The Queen Anne-style Valentine Building (202 Front Street) was constructed in 1904 and 1913 by Emery Valentine, a jeweler and prominent civic leader. On the National Register of Historic Places, it was restored in 1982. If you drop in at the drugstore, check out the ornate gilded ceiling.

One of downtown Juneau's two ATMs is at the First National Bank, 238 Front Street. 🏧

🚶 *Turn right on Seward Street and proceed up the hill one block.*

**⓫** At Second and Seward Streets, the five-story **Goldstein Building** originated in 1914 as fur buyer Charles Goldstein's department store. The building also housed the second and third Territorial Legislatures.

To the left is the **Messerschmidt Building** (120 Second Street). There has been a bakery on this site since 1890. The current building, constructed in 1914, was a bakery for years and is now the Silverbow Inn and Restaurant, which also runs a bakery.
✗ SILVERBOW INN AND RESTAURANT

Downtown's other ATM is at National Bank of Alaska, at the corner of Seward and Second Streets. 🆂

🚶 *Cross Second Street and continue up one block to Third Street.*

A U.S. Postal Station is at 221 Seward Street; Olivia's Mexican Restaurant is downstairs at 222 Seward Street. ✉ ✗ OLIVIA'S MEXICAN RESTAURANT

**⓬** The **Davis Log Cabin** (Third and Seward Streets; (907) 586-2201) is the Juneau Convention & Visitors Bureau's main visitor information center. This is the best place to get the low-down on what there is to see and do in Juneau. Or just drop in for a cup of coffee and chat with the staff.

The log cabin replica was built by volunteers in 1980 for Juneau's Centennial. It's named for Juneau pioneer J. Montgomery Davis, a bookkeeper who arrived from London, England, in 1891, and his wife, Frances, a painter and also a Londoner. They were married in the original building when it was the city's first Presbyterian Church. It later housed the first public school and then a brewery.

## FISH AND OTHER AIRBORNE HAZARDS

Juneau has the distinction of being the location of the only recorded mid-air collision between a jet and a steelhead. On the morning of March 31, 1987, an Alaska Airlines Boeing 737 was taking off from Juneau International Airport. The ascending jet crossed paths with a bald eagle that had just caught its breakfast: a steelhead trout. The startled eagle dropped its fish, which smacked into the airplane with a "thud" as the eagle flew off unharmed. The jet was inspected at its next stop and found to be undamaged by its close encounter with the fish. As the airline's employee publication put it: "The sole crime was slime." The fish story attracted national attention, though, especially since the next day was April Fools.

🚶 *From the Davis Log Cabin, turn right along Third Street one block to Main Street. Turn right up the hill.*

**13** At mid-block there's a life-sized bronze sculpture of a brown bear, **"Windfall Fisherman,"** created by Juneau artist R.T. "Skip" Wallen. It's in the courtyard of the **Dimond Courthouse**, named for John H. Dimond (1918–1985), justice of the original Supreme Court of Alaska.

From the sculpture, there's an excellent view of the marble-columned Alaska State Capitol. 📷

🚶 *Continue up the hill and cross Fourth Street to the Capitol Building.*

**14** **Alaska's State Capitol** was built in 1931 as the Federal and Territorial Building, using marble mined

at Tokeen on Prince of Wales Island near Ketchikan. Marble lines the lobby; there's also a marble bear sculpture. The Liberty Bell replica in front of the building was donated to the state during a savings bond drive.

Free, 20-minute guided tours are available at a desk in the lobby during the summer. The Governor's Office is on the third floor. The Alaska State Legislature meets on the second floor beginning in January. Floor sessions start about 11 a.m. weekdays. Visitor galleries for House and Senate are on the second floor. 🚻

🚶 *After exiting the Capitol Building, proceed left half a block to Seward Street, turn left for a fairly steep block to Fifth Street, then turn right for a block and a half.*

**⑮** On the National Register of Historic Places, **St. Nicholas Russian Orthodox Church** (1894) is the oldest original Russian Orthodox church in Southeast Alaska. The small (27-foot diameter) octagonal building symbolizes the seven days of the week and an "eighth day" of rest. Its entry is on the opposite side from the street to conform with a church dictate that the altar be placed toward the east. Photographs are permitted inside the church, which has many beau-

tiful works of art, including eighteenth-century icons. The church is open for tours weekdays from 9 a.m. to 6 p.m.; a $1 donation is requested. Visitors are welcome to attend Sunday services at 10 a.m. year-round 📷

🚶 *After exiting the church, return to Fifth Street and turn left. Proceed to the corner and turn left up Gold Street for two very steep blocks to Seventh Street and turn left.*

OPTION:

🚶 *For a detour to Starr Hill, turn to the right on Sixth Street. From Gold Street, walk three steep blocks to Kennedy Street.*

**Starr Hill** is one of Juneau's oldest neighborhoods, named for early-day builder Frank Starr. Kennedy Street is the namesake of Irish immigrant Dan Kennedy, who arrived in Juneau in 1880 and served for many years as Juneau's night watchman and constable.

*Left, top:* Ladies and gents will find a frontier-style welcome at the Red Dog Saloon. *Left, bottom:* View up North Franklin Street; flags fly on the front of the Baranof Hotel. *Top:* Find out about Juneau sightseeing and more at the Davis Log Cabin. *Above:* The six Kennedy Street mineworkers houses were built in 1913 to house miners' families. *Right:* "Windfall Fisherman" graces the courtyard of the Dimond Courthouse.

At the corner of Sixth and Kennedy is **Chicken Yard Park**, with a small sculpture of a nun feeding chickens. Now a playground, it once was the chicken yard for a convent.

Many of Starr Hill's homes were built to be rented to mining families. The **Kennedy Street Mineworkers Houses**, six formerly identical Craftsman-style bungalows on Kennedy between Sixth and Fifth, are prime examples. Built in 1913, the homes have taken on individual looks through the years.

A bit farther along Kennedy, at Fifth Street, is a charming wooden sculpture of children linking arms in a circle. Titled **"Living Together in Peace,"** it sits near the top of a stairway from Kennedy down to East Streets.

*🚶 Return to Gold Street either by taking the stairway down to East Street and then walking right to Sixth or by walking back on Kennedy and then down Sixth Street.*

**16** The **Chicken Ridge** area along Seventh, Goldbelt, and Dixon Streets (plus the upper portion of Main Street between Sixth and Seventh) is another of Juneau's oldest neighborhoods. It was named by early-day miners, who hunted grouse and ptarmigan ("chickens" to them) in the area. The ridge separates the Evergreen Bowl/Cope Park recreation area and downtown Juneau. Numerous large, turn-of-the-century homes dot the neighborhood. An effort is under way to nominate it as a Historic District.

*🚶 Continue one and a half blocks to 213 Seventh Street.*

**17** The **Wickersham House** (213 Seventh Street) was built in 1899 for Frank Hammond, superintendent of the Sheep Creek Mining Co. In 1928, the home was purchased by Judge James Wickersham, a noted Alaskan lawyer, politician, historian, author, and statehood proponent, who lived here until his

---

### JUNEAU BEAR-Y TALES

For all its sophistication, Alaska's capital city is literally at the edge of the wilderness. There's wildlife galore, but the black bears that regularly wander into town get the most attention. (Seems Juneau was built on an historic bear migration route and the bears haven't forgotten they were here first.) In 1994, police responded to 37 incidents of bear/human encounters. In 1993, a bear appeared at the front door of a downtown supermarket. And, in 1991, a cub wandered into the hospital's emergency room.

Local TV announcements warn about "garbage bears." One downtown neighborhood has "bear monitors" who ensure the animals' "safe passage" or call the police if necessary. Residents commonly put their garbage in the freezer until pickup day so it doesn't attract bears. And "out the road" in the Mendenhall Valley, an ultra-heavy-duty fence surrounds an elementary school—not to keep the kids in, but to keep the bears out.

---

death in 1939. As Alaska's third delegate to Congress, Wickersham worked to obtain a territorial legislature (1912), a federal (now private) railroad linking Anchorage and Fairbanks (1914), and Mount McKinley National Park and the agricultural college that later became the University of Alaska (1917). On the National Register of Historic Places, the home is owned  by the State of Alaska. The nonprofit Wickersham Society operates tours in the summer.

Next door, at 227 Seventh Street, is the Faulkner House, a Colonial Revival-style home built in 1914 for Herbert Faulkner, a deputy U.S. marshal and lawyer.

Across the street, at 206 Seventh Street, is the Thane-Holbrook House, a bungalow built c.1916 for Bartlett Thane, manager and director of the Alaska Gastineau Mining Co.

Around the corner from the Wickersham House is a public stairway—the Seward Street Stairs—down to Sixth and Fifth Streets. (Please respect adjoining private property.) Trees obscure the view from the top of the stairs.

*Left, top:* Alaska's governor often strolls to work along the Calhoun Avenue Promenade from the white-columned Governor's Mansion. *Left, bottom:* Nasturtiums brighten Juneau residence on Gastineau Avenue. *Top:* Turn-of-the-century homes along Gastineau Avenue. *Bottom:* Floatplanes are part of the scene along Juneau's bustling waterfront; Douglas Island is in the background.

👥 *From the Wickersham House continue along Seventh to Main Street and turn left down the hill.*

---

OPTION: Before heading down Main Street, detour for a **great view**.

👥 *Cross Main and continue on Seventh, which curves and becomes Goldbelt Avenue. Go another half a block to the West Eighth Street Stairs.*

From the stairs, you'll have a view of Douglas Island, Gastineau Channel, the Juneau-Douglas Bridge, and West Juneau. 📷

---

👥 *Retrace your steps back to Seventh and Main.*

**18** The **intersection of Seventh and Main** is a great spot from which to take photos. From here, you can easily see why Juneau is often referred to as "**Little San Francisco.**" 📷

On Main Street hill, you'll pass through a picturesque neighborhood with some of the oldest homes in Juneau. Most porches and yards are bright with flowers in the summer.

👥 *Continue downhill to Fifth Street and turn right half a block.*

**19** From the center of the **footbridge over Calhoun Avenue**, there's an excellent view of the Governor's Mansion, the Calhoun Avenue Promenade (built in 1995), Gastineau Channel, the Juneau-Douglas Bridge, and Douglas Island. 📷

Calhoun Avenue follows a trail that once linked downtown Juneau with the Auke Indian community, over the side of the hill. The street was named for Juneau pioneers John and Mary Calhoun, whose dairy was on the site of the Governor's Mansion.

🚶 *Retrace your steps back to Main Street and turn right down the hill to Fourth Street.*

**❷⓪** The **Juneau-Douglas City Museum**, on the corner of Fourth and Main Streets, has an extensive collection of mining relics and other artifacts. A "Welcome Back to the Past" room offers "hands-on" history for kids of all ages. An 8-by-5-foot relief map orients visitors to Juneau's
topography. Videos tell about the founding of Juneau and Douglas and helpful staff and volunteers answer questions. The Museum Shop sells books, souvenirs, and collectibles.

Open daily mid-May to mid–Sept.; 9 a.m.–5 p.m. weekdays; 11 a.m.–5 p.m. weekends. Mid-Sept. to mid-May, open Thurs.–Sat., noon to 4:30 p.m.; other times by appointment. Admission: Adults $1; children under 18 free. Free admission on Saturdays from mid-Sept. to mid-May. 🚻 ♿

🚶 *After leaving the museum, cross Fourth Street and continue to the right to the large building.*

**❷①** The 11-story **State Office Building** was constructed in 1974, nestled into the side of Courthouse Hill, named for the federal court-house that stood here from 1903 until the early 1970s. Known locally as "The SOB," it houses the **Alaska State Library**, including the state's historical library (hours are 8 a.m. to 5 p.m. weekdays), as well as state offices. From Fourth Street, enter a
large atrium housing the **Old Witch Totem Pole**, carved in the late 1800s, and an antique **Kimball pipe organ**, a reminder of the silent films that enter-tained early-day Juneauites. Drop in for the free organ concert at noon each Friday.

The large terrace on the opposite side of the building affords excellent views. 📷

### TOWN WHERE THE TAKUS BLOW

During the fall and winter, Juneauites experience one of Alaska's more infamous weather phenomena: the taku winds. Bone-chilling takus scream down off the Juneau Icefield at up to 100 miles per hour, packing enough power to have once punched a 2-by-4 board through the wall of a house. Because of the accompanying power outages, every local resident has at least one Thanksgiving or Christmas Day storm story, complete with details on how they cooked the turkey during the power outage.

The elevators at the back of the atrium are the quickest way to get from "upper Juneau" at the Fourth Street level to "lower Juneau" at the Willoughby Avenue level. Keep in mind, though, that the building is locked on weekends. 🚻

🚶 *Exit the State Office Building from the Fourth Street doors (where you came in) and turn left on Fourth, which curves and becomes Calhoun Avenue. Continue for two blocks along the Calhoun Avenue Promenade, which has benches and good views.* 📷

**22** At the corner of Calhoun Avenue and Distin Street is the Colonial Revival-style **Governor's Mansion**, listed on the National Register of Historic Places. The official residence of Alaska's governor, the home was built in 1912, the year Alaska became a territory of the United States and Juneau was named its capital. The Governor's Totem Pole was carved in 1940 by Charlie Tagook and William Brown of Klukwan and Saxman. The original building cost $40,000, including furniture. In 1983, extensive renovations returned the mansion to its original decor—at a cost of $2 million. No regular tours of the mansion are offered; however, there's a public open house in early December and private tours may be arranged through the Office of the Governor (call (907) 465-3500 for information).

🚶 *Retrace your steps back on Calhoun to the pedestrian over-pass. Take the 90 stairs down to Willoughby Avenue. Or, go back to the State Office Building and all the way through the atrium, then take the elevator down to Willoughby (weekday option only). Once you're on Willoughby, turn to the right for 2 to 5 minutes, depending on which option you chose, around a curve to Whittier Street and turn left one block.*

About a block past Whittier, at 429 W. Willoughby Ave. is the Fiddlehead Restaurant. ✗ FIDDLEHEAD RESTAURANT

OPTION:
🚶 *Continue past the Governor's Mansion on Calhoun Avenue, downhill for about 5 minutes. Calhoun becomes Irwin Street on the other side of Gold Creek. Follow Irwin as it veers to the right, into the entrance of the cemetery.*

**Evergreen Cemetery** is the resting place of many Juneau pioneers, including the city's co-founders, Joseph Juneau and Richard T. Harris, who lie buried across the path from each other about 3 minutes into the cemetery. On other graves, you may recognize names from Juneau's streets and historic buildings.

🚶 *Continue through the cemetery for another five minutes to Glacier Avenue and turn left.*

Facing Glacier Avenue is a monument to **Clan Leader Kowee** of the Auke Tribe, who led Juneau and Harris to the October 1880 gold discovery that led to the settlement of the city of Juneau. The monument marks the approximate location were Kowee's body was cremated according to Tlingit custom of the time.

🚶 *Retrace your steps back through the cemetery, on Irwin and Calhoun, past the Governor's Mansion to the pedestrian overpass.*

❷❸ The **Alaska State Museum** (392 Whittier Street), built in 1967 on fill from mine "tailings," has an

> ## THE BIRD MAN OF JUNEAU
>
> One night in 1909, a man was shot and killed in Juneau. Not an uncommon event in a rough-and-tumble mining town. But this shooting was committed by one Robert Stroud, whose later crimes earned him a life sentence at Alcatraz Federal Penitentiary in San Francisco Bay, where he became known as "The Bird Man of Alcatraz" because of his dedication to learning about and caring for birds.
>
> Stroud killed the bartender from the Alaskan Hotel at a little house that used to stand behind what is now the American Legion Hall, at the corner of Fourth and Franklin Streets.

excellent collection of Alaskana, featuring the state's Native cultures, Russian history, mining and fishing history, a wildlife display, and traveling exhibits.

Begun as a territorial museum in 1900, the museum now has more than 25,000 artifacts and works of art. Its two floors are connected by a ramp that curves around an atrium and an "eagle tree," an exhibit including a nest and seven bald eagles at various life stages. Other natural history exhibits along the ramp include totem poles, a petroglyph, plant life, and brown bears. The Museum Shop sells Alaska Native art, publications, graphics, and educational products.

On the lawn is "Nimbus," a modern sculpture that generated much controversy when it was originally installed in front of the Dimond Courthouse. The Legislature ordered it moved.

Open daily mid-May to mid-Sept.; 9 a.m.–6 p.m. weekdays; 10 a.m.–6 p.m. weekends. Mid-September to mid-May open Tues.–Sat.; 10 a.m.–4 p.m. Admission: adults $3; children 18 and under, and students with current ID cards, free. Free guided tours offered during the summer. 🚻 ♿

🚶 *From the museum, continue to the right on Whittier Street to Egan Drive and turn left for a block to the convention center.*

**24** The **U.S. Forest Service Information Center** is located in the lobby of **Centennial Hall**, at 101 Egan Drive (named for Alaska's first governor, William A.

Egan). You can find information about the Tongass National Forest, Forest Service cabins, hiking opportunities and other outdoor activities, films about the area's flora and fauna, informational displays, and natural history books. (Phone: (907) 586-8751.) 🚻 ♿

Across from Centennial Hall is "**the subport,**" named for the submarines that docked there during World War II. Now it's home to the U.S. Coast Guard and National Marine Fisheries Service.

🚶 *From Centennial Hall, it's 3 blocks to the end of the walking tour. Turn left on Egan Drive, which becomes Marine Way at Main Street.*

OPTION:

🚶 *Turn left at Main Street and walk three blocks to West Third Street, turn left and go up the hill.*

**Telephone Hill** was named after William Webster, who placed Juneau's first telephone line across Gastineau Channel in 1883, connecting his home (Juneau's oldest, built in 1882) on top of the hill to his store in Douglas. The Webster family ran the telephone company until the 1950s.

🚶 *West Third curves and becomes Dixon Street. Continue about 2 blocks to a dead end.*

The end of Dixon has good views of the channel, boat and floatplane traffic, and cruise ships. 📷

🚶 *Continue to the left, down a set of stairs. Turn right on Main Street for a block back to Marine Way and turn left.*

㉕ At Main Street and Marine Way is the headquarters of the **Sealaska Corporation,** one of 12 regional corporations formed under the Alaska Native Claims Settlement Act of 1971.

🚶 *Walk 2 blocks back to Marine Park and the end of the walking tour.*

*Above:* Craggy peak jutting from the Juneau Ice Cap is part of the Coast Range. *Right, top:* Rafters enjoy a sunny day on the Mendenhall River. *Right, bottom:* Mendenhall Glacier is a top attraction with visitors.

# Getting Out of Town

### HIGH ON THE VIEW: MOUNT ROBERTS TRAMWAY

Soar with the eagles 2,000 feet above Juneau aboard the Mount Roberts Tramway. Two 60-person cars depart every 12 to 15 minutes from the terminal at the cruise ship dock.

The tramway runs up the mountain to a weather-protected observation deck with panoramic views. Other attractions include a restaurant, Native crafts shop, and a theater featuring a film about Southeast Alaska Native cultures. Tram rates are $15.95 for adults; $9.95 for children 6–12; children under 6, free.

### TAKE A HIKE: MOUNT ROBERTS TRAIL

One of Juneau's most accessible trails is the one up Mount Roberts, which begins on Starr Hill at the east end of Sixth Street. The trail ascends 4.5 miles to the 3,819-foot summit for spectacular views. It is moderately difficult, but well maintained, with plenty of places to stop off and enjoy the view. For a quickie wilderness experience and a great photo opportunity, there's an excellent viewpoint about 20 minutes up. (See page vii for hiking cautions.)

### TAKE A HIKE: BASIN ROAD
### AND LAST CHANCE MINING MUSEUM

Basin Road offers a level, mile-long hike into the hills behind Juneau to Last Chance Basin. Walk up Gold Street to the top, turn right, then left at the next corner onto Basin Road. At the end of the dirt road, go right over a footbridge. The Last Chance Mining Museum is in the old compressor house of the Alaska-Juneau Gold Mining Co. It has the original 11-ton compressor wheel and much more equipment. (Other mine buildings are in disrepair and should not be entered.) Admission is $3. Museum hours may be irregular; call (907) 586-5338 for information or for an appointment.

### JUNEAU'S BACKYARD GLACIER: MENDENHALL

Just 13 miles from downtown, Juneau's backyard glacier, Mendenhall, is an awe-inspiring sight. A frozen river

12 miles long, 1½ miles wide, and a hundred feet deep, Mendenhall emanates from the 1,500-square-mile Juneau Icefield, located just over the mountains behind the city. The visitors center features an excellent view of the glacier's face, telescopes for a close-up look, a three-dimensional topographical map of the entire icefield, guided nature hikes, and video programs. Call (907) 789-0097 or 586-8800 for information.

You can drive from Juneau to the glacier via the Glacier Highway and Mendenhall Loop Road. Or, take a Capital Transit bus to the Mendenhall Glacier Spur Road and from there, walk the 1.4 miles to the visitors center. (Information available at the Davis Log Cabin Information Center, 134 Third St., or from the bus company, (907) 789-6901.) You can also hire a taxi for a flat rate (Taku Taxi, (907) 586-2121, or Capital Cab, (907) 586-2772).

Several flightseeing and helicopter operators offer the chance to view, or even walk on, the icefield. Also, a visit to Mendenhall Glacier is included on most city tours (available on board cruise ships). Call Gray Line of Alaska, (907) 586-3773, for city tour information; Wings of Alaska, (907) 586-8258, for flightseeing; Temsco Helicopters, (907) 789-9501, or ERA Helicopters, (907) 586-2030, for heli-touring.

### ICEBERG EXTRAVAGANZA: GLACIER BAY NATIONAL PARK

Two hundred years ago, when Captain George Vancouver was exploring the area, Glacier Bay was just a dent in a 4,000-foot-thick wall of ice along the shore of Icy Strait, 50 miles from Juneau. Today, visitors can travel 60 miles up the bay from the park headquarters at Bartlett Cove, viewing 12 tidewater glaciers along the way. This 3.3-million-acre park also features humpback whales, harbor seals, and a multitude of birds.

For information, contact Glacier Bay National Park and Preserve, (907) 697-2230; Glacier Bay Tours and Cruises, (800) 451-5952; or check with the Davis Log Cabin Information Center, 134 Third St., Juneau. Many cruise ships visit Glacier Bay.

# Skagway at a Glance

**Population:** City of Skagway: 767 (5.5% Alaska Natives); 1,300 in summer, with seasonal workers 52.5% Men; 47.5% Women Visitors: 500,000 + annually

**Geography:** City of Skagway: 454.7 sq. mi. Location: At the head of Taiya Inlet at the northernmost end of Lynn Canal on the mainland of Southeast Alaska, 15 highway miles south of the U.S./Canada border, 95 air miles northeast of Juneau and nearly 1,000 air miles north of Seattle

**Weather:** Average summer temperatures: 45-67°F Average winter temperatures: 18 to 37°F Annual precipitation: 29"

**Primary Industries:** Tourism ($40 million industry) Retail shops and services Government Railroad (operated seasonally) Trans-shipment of freight, fuel and lead/zinc ore

**Facilities and Services:** Skagway School (about 130 students, grades K-12 only); Skagway Medical Service health clinic (nearest hospital is in Juneau); Newspaper: biweekly *Skagway News*. One cable TV service. Radio: KHNS-FM 91.9.

**Visitor Information:** Skagway Visitors Bureau, on 5th between Broadway and State, (907) 983-2855. Loads of information on what to see and do in Skagway. Klondike Gold Rush National Historical Park Visitors Center, Second and Broadway, (907) 983-2921. Information, programs, and displays on the gold rush, hiking the Chilkoot Trail. Open May-September only.

# Skagway

*"We are a living historical community.
We didn't recreate Broadway in some kind
of urban renewal project."*
—Skagway resident

The Klondike Gold Rush gave birth to Skagway in a two-year frenzy, during which a handful of homesteaders exploded into as many as 15,000 gold-crazed stampeders. And the gold rush keeps Skagway alive today. These days, however, the stampeders come from cruise ships and ferries.

Skagway is the genuine article. "We are a living historical community. We didn't recreate Broadway in some kind of urban renewal project," says a local. Narrow, false-fronted buildings line Broadway's boardwalks. Many structures in the 6-by-2-block historic district are original; a few are even said to harbor ghosts. Strolling the boardwalks, you can imagine lively tunes from a honky-tonk piano, the clamor of a thousand excited voices, maybe a gunshot or two—echoes of the past in this historic "Gateway to the Klondike."

Summer is Skagway's season. And when it's over, the town shuts down. Only a few businesses stay open during the winter months, and nearly a third of the population leaves town for warmer climes. "After 14- and 16-hour days in the summer, they just want to kick back," explains a resident.

Once, only the hunting camps of the Chilkoot Tlingits were here. The Chilkoots zealously guarded access to the steep, rugged route over Chilkoot Pass, the ancient "grease trail" used for trading oily hooligan fish for furs and copper from the Tagish Athabaskans in the interior. When the trail was opened to others in 1880, the Chilkoots quickly adapted, securing the lucrative business of packing prospectors' outfits over the pass.

Early in 1887, Captain William "Billy" Moore bushwhacked his way along a "secret" route up the Skagway River valley and White Pass was opened. Moore was convinced it would be the primary route to the Yukon, where he predicted a major gold strike would occur. In anticipation, he built a cabin, sawmill, and wharf on Skagway Bay.

*"Although Skagway's population officially is 52.5% male and 47.5% female, in the winter it seems more like 15 or 16 men to each woman."*

Nothing much happened until 1896, when three prospectors—"Skookum" Jim Mason, George Washington Carmack, and Tagish Charlie—made an incredibly rich gold strike on a tributary of the Klondike River. It was the middle of nowhere—but not for long. Local prospectors poured in, staking the creeks feeding the Klondike. But it was nearly a year before news of the strike reached the outside world.

On July 15, 1897, a ship steamed into San Francisco bearing a couple of dozen prospectors and their gold. Two days later, another ship arrived in Seattle, this time with 68 miners. And the world took notice. "A ton of gold!" trumpeted a local newspaper. All of North America, then in the depths of a severe economic depression, was electrified. By nightfall, the great Klondike Gold Rush had begun.

Gold-crazed men and women booked passage for the Klondike, even though most had no idea where it was. Seattle, a frontier outpost of about 67,000, lost 10,000 residents that first summer, but prosperity soon doubled its population as merchants sold all manner of goods to the "argonauts."

The first boatload of stampeders hit Skagway on July 29. Overnight, a tent city sprang up. With only one U.S. deputy marshal in the entire region, Skagway was a lawless town. A commander of Canada's North West Mounted Police dubbed it "the roughest place in the world, little better than a hell on earth." It boasted some 70 saloons, brothels did a brisk business, shootings were commonplace. Jefferson Randolph "Soapy" Smith and his gang held sway for several months, until Smith died in a famous shootout with town surveyor Frank Reid.

By the spring of 1898, tramways crossed Chilkoot Pass, and Brackett's Wagon Road approached the summit of White Pass. Around the same time, a deal was struck to build the White Pass & Yukon Route. With its completion, Chilkoot Pass no longer needed.

Then, as quickly as it had begun, the gold rush was over. With its end

*Although Alaska had been "dry" since its purchase from Russia, Gold Rush-era Skagway boasted 70 saloons and 3 breweries.*

in 1900, Skagway might have become a ghost town if not for the WP&YR, which provided a vital connection to Whitehorse and mines in the Yukon. The railroad was Skagway's economic mainstay until 1982, when it shut down. The little town of Skagway was brought to its knees. "They laid off 185 people and within two years 400 people lost their jobs," recalls a former employee.

Tourism saved Skagway. In 1976, Congress had created Klondike Gold Rush National Historical Park, and restoration of Skagway's gold rush-era buildings, many of which were boarded up and in danger of falling down, began in earnest. Then, in 1988, the WP&YR reopened as an excursion train.

Today, the historic buildings—many housing bustling shops and restaurants—have been colorfully restored. Bountiful gardens boost Skagway's fame as the "Garden City of Alaska." More than 500,000 visitors come each

*Above:* Visitors board a helicopter on Skagway's waterfront for a flight-seeing tour. *Right, top:* The Golden North Hotel is reputed to harbor a gold rush-era ghost. *Right, bottom:* Steam locomotive of the White Pass & Yukon Route chuffs along near the waterfront.

summer. Tourism has expanded to offer backcountry hiking, mountain biking, and other "soft adventure" tours. The

shipment of ore, fuel, and freight via the Klondike Highway to and from Canada bolsters the economy.

Its isolation and the seasonal nature of its economy lend a zany zest to life in Skagway. Says one local, "People get a little crazy and do things like a chainsaw-throwing contest or bowling on Broadway. The imagination in this town is a wonderful thing."

## FESTIVALS AND OTHER FUN

Skagway happenings of note include: Windfest, a "cabin fever reliever," with such events as a canoe race on snow, and the Buckwheat Ski Classic, both in March; the Mini-Folk Festival in mid-April; Summer Solstice Party and Midnight Picnic; Soapy Smith's Wake every July 8; the Eastern Star Flower Show and Gold Rush Garden Club Competition in August; the Klondike Trail of '98 Road Relay Race from Skagway to Whitehorse in September; and the "Victorian Yuletide" celebration

*Skagway is like a big shopping mall —it's an easy town and a flat town.*

and ball in early December. For more, look in the *Skagway News* or call the Skagway Convention and Visitors Bureau at (907) 983-2855.

## DON'T MISS

Skagway attractions not to miss:

- The Klondike Gold Rush Historical Park visitors center (Stop #1 on the walking tour), for giant photographs and excellent displays about the gold rush days.
- The Golden North Hotel (Stop #5), with its funky lobby and a big photo of Skagway in the winter.
- The Red Onion (Stop #3), for ragtime music and a local crowd.

- A ride on the White Pass & Yukon Route (Stop #1), where you can travel in comfort aboard vintage railroad cars and imagine what the stampeders endured making their way over the pass.

## GRABBING A BITE
Following are a few suggested dining spots. The number indicates where to look for them along the walking tour.

- Lorna's at the Skagway Inn, 655 Broadway (Stop #11). Le Cordon Bleu fine dining. In Skagway, no less! Reservations suggested, (907) 983-3161. Menu changes daily. Dinner nightly May–September. Wine and beer. $$$$
- Sweet Tooth Cafe, Broadway and Third (Stop #5). Cheerful, comfortable, casual. Sandwiches on home-made bread. Train box lunches. Open all year; 6 a.m.–2 p.m. in winter, 6 a.m.–9 p.m. in summer. $
- Portland House Restaurant & Inn, 5th and State Streets (Stop #9). International, eclectic menu: American, Mexican, Italian, and Greek. Beer and wine. Open 11 a.m.–11 p.m. $–$$

## STOP TO SHOP
Most shops line Broadway and side streets in the central downtown area. A few suggested places to stop and shop:

- David Present Gallery, Broadway and Third. Unique jewelry, pottery, rare woods, contemporary Alaskan carvings. Seasonal.
- Jim Stamper Jewelry, on Third next to the Present Gallery. Specializes in jewelry made from old silver coins that are flattened, polished, and pierced with Alaskan designs. Seasonal.
- Kirmse's Curio Store, Broadway and Fifth. Established in 1897 and hasn't changed much since then. See Soapy Smith's pistol and the world's largest and smallest gold nugget watch chains. Gold nugget jewelry is still made right here. Seasonal.
- Lynch & Kennedy Dry Goods, 350 Broadway. Native and locally made artworks, hand-painted T-shirts, custom jewelry, home accessories. Open all year.

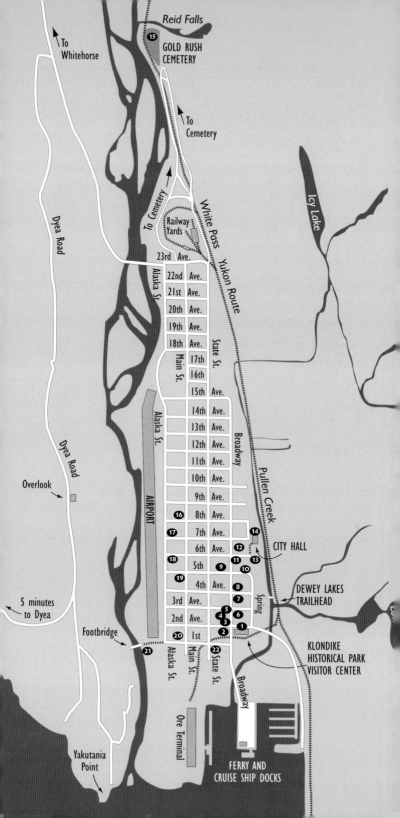

# The Walking Tour

**1** Klondike National Historical Park Visitor Center, page 82.

**2** Jeff. Smiths Parlor, page 86.

**3** Red Onion Saloon, page 87.

**4** Arctic Brotherhood Hall; Trail of '98 Skagway Historical Museum, page 87.

**5** Golden North Hotel, page 89.

**6** The Mascot Saloon, page 90.

**7** Pack Train Building, page 91.

**8** St. James Hotel, page 91.

**9** Skagway Visitors Bureau, page 94.

**10** The Moore Cabin; White Pass Trail, page 94.

**11** Eagles Hall; "Days of '98" show, page 95.

**12** Mollie Walsh Park, page 95.

**13** Pullen House ruins, page 98.

**14** Skagway City Hall (McCabe College), page 99.

**15** Gold Rush Cemetery, page 100.

**16** The White House, page 101.

**17** The Nye House; Case-Mulvihill House, page 101.

**18** The Gault House, page 102.

**19** First Presbyterian Church, page 102.

**20** WP&YR housing, page 102.

**21** Yakutania Point, page 103.

**22** Memorial mountain ash trees; Frank Reid-Soapy Smith shootout marker, page 103.

# Skagway Walking Tour

S kagway is a compact, flat town that's great for walking. This tour takes you through the main shopping area and historic district. You'll see displays about gold rush history at both the Klondike Gold Rush National Historical Park visitor center and the Trail of '98 Museum, a White Pass & Yukon Route engine, a monument to the "Angel of White Pass," and take a side trip to the Gold Rush Cemetery. Estimated time is 1½ hours for the majority of the walking tour, depending on stops, plus another 1½ hours round trip to the cemetery.

**1** This walking tour starts at the **Klondike National Historical Park Visitor Center** in the former White Pass & Yukon Route depot, a reddish building with cream-gold trim, on the corner of Broadway Street and Second Avenue.

🚶 *From anywhere downtown, head down Broadway toward the waterfront. The visitor center is to the left on the corner at Second Avenue.*

🚶 *From the ferry terminal or the cruise ship docks, head toward the center of the pier area and walk into town on Broadway. The park visitor center is to the right at Second Avenue.*

Coming from the piers, you'll see a large information kiosk that will help orient you to downtown Skagway.

The old White Pass & Yukon Route depot (1898) and the adjacent cream-and-black WP&YR railroad office building (1900) were used until 1969, when a new depot was built next door (that's where you catch the train today). The old depot is now owned by the National Park Service, which offers a number of free programs during the summer including a ranger-guided tour of the historic district; a 30-minute film, "Days of Adventure, Dreams of Gold"; and ranger talks on a variety of subjects. Displays include a bronze plaque dedicated to the thousands of pack animals that died on White Pass during the Klondike Gold Rush; a representation of the "ton of goods" that each miner had to haul over the passes; a reproduction of the historic newspaper front page

## SKAGWAY'S STILL SOAPY'S TOWN

In some ways, Skagway is still Soapy Smith's town. The "Days of '98" show celebrates his nefarious feats. "Soapy," the actor, glad-hands visitors. Soapy's saloon still stands on Second Street (Stop #2). Although he operated for less than a year, Soapy Smith's legend lives on.

Jefferson Randolph "Soapy" Smith earned his con-artist reputation selling $1 bars of soap, some of which supposedly were wrapped in $5 to $50 bills. However, only his shills ever "won" a big bill. Arriving in lawless Skagway in the fall of 1897, Soapy and his gang established a saloon and gambling house, Jeff. Smiths Parlor, and preyed on prospectors with various swindles, a protection racket, and robbery. A notorious venture was his "Telegraph Office," which charged $5 (a significant sum in those days) to send a message. "Responses" arrived in a few hours, always collect. Business boomed, even though Skagway had no telegraph lines at the time.

Things came to a head on July 7, 1898, when miner John Douglas Stewart "lost" his $2,700 gold poke after two strangers encouraged him to leave it in a hotel safe overnight. Stewart complained loudly all over town, prompting the vigilante Committee of 101 (formed to squelch Smith) to demand the return of Stewart's money. Smith disavowed knowledge of the matter. The next night, a drunken and armed Smith appeared at a pier where the committee was meeting and challenged surveyor Frank Reid, one of four men standing guard. Shots were exchanged. Smith wounded Reid in the groin; Reid fired three shots, one through Smith's heart.

Smith died on the dock. Reid died 12 days later, acclaimed as Skagway's hero. Reid's grave at the Gold Rush Cemetery has an imposing granite monument. Nearby, adorned with a simple marker, is Smith's grave, just outside the cemetery boundary. Ironically, each July 8, Skagway commemorates the outlaw, not the hero, with "Soapy Smith's Wake," complete with champagne provided by Soapy's descendants.

*Top:* The rollicking Red Onion Saloon, left, and the Klondike Gold Rush Historical Park Visitors Center, right. *Bottom:* Intricate driftwood facade decorates the Arctic Brotherhood building, which houses the Trail of '98 Museum. *Right:* Soapy Smith's weathered headstone.

trumpeting the arrival of the first miners in Seattle; and enlargements of historic photographs of early-day Skagway and the stampeders. Information on hiking the Chilkoot Trail is available at the information desk. Open 8 a.m.–6 p.m. daily, late May and September; 8 a.m.–8 p.m. daily June, July, and August. For information, call (907) 983-2921. 🏛 ♿

---

### SKAGWAY'S BIG MAC MEDIVAC

On February 13, 1982, all of Skagway experienced a Big Mac attack of epic proportions.

The first McDonald's in Juneau had just opened and amid the fast-food frenzy occasioned by this event, the burghers of Skagway set about arranging a community order of burgers to be airlifted 95 miles northward. According to a local paper, the feast included 200 orders of fries, 150 Big Macs, and 50 Quarter Pounders. The community bill came to around $800—about a dollar for every resident.

Nearly 200 people braved a wind chill factor of 40 below zero to await the arrival of the "Mac Attack Medivacs." After some initial freeze-up problems with their instruments, the school band serenaded the assemblage. Finally, 45 minutes late, two red cross-emblazoned Medivac planes rolled down the runway with a police escort, blue and red lights flashing. Wearing hospital greens, the pilots hustled the food into the terminal for distribution, while the band played "Old Mac-Donald Had a Farm."

Just what the doctor ordered to cure a bad case of cabin fever.

---

🚶 *From the visitors center, turn left and cross Broadway to the second building from the corner.*

**❷ Jeff. Smiths Parlor** was built in 1897 as Skagway's first bank. After arriving in 1897, the notorious outlaw Jefferson Randolph "Soapy" Smith and his henchmen operated a saloon and gambling hall in this building. Originally located on Sixth Avenue at Broadway Street (where the Bank of Alaska now stands), it has been relocated twice and a couple of additions have been tacked on. However, the front still looks much as it did during the gold rush. Soapy was shot around the corner—there's a marker at First and State indicating the approximate location (Stop #22).

👫 *Head back to Broadway, turn left and cross Second.*

❸ Broadway passes through the **main shopping area** and the heart of the 6-block-long **historic district**. Most of the buildings in the historic district—bounded roughly by Second and Seventh Avenues on the south and north, and by State and Spring Streets to the west and east—are original, constructed from 1897 to 1900. However, from 1900 to 1915 some were relocated to the central area when Skagway was shrinking in size after the gold rush.

On the northwest corner of Second and Broadway is the **Red Onion Saloon**. Built in 1898, it was a dance hall and saloon, with a brothel upstairs. On the back bar there was a doll representing each "working girl." When she was with a client, the doll reclined; it was upright when she wasn't busy. The money paid upstairs—preferably in gold—was dropped through slots in the floor for safekeeping by the bartender. Mannequins peering from the upstairs windows give a sense of the days when the "girls" were in residence. The bar also is reputed to have a ghost.

👫 *Proceed up Broadway half a block.*

You'll pass the former Washington Fruit Store (built in 1899 by the Rapuzzis, a pioneer Skagway family) and the 1900 building that originally housed the Washington & Alaska Steamship Co. office. A gift shop now occupies both buildings.

❹ Three doors up from the Red Onion is "the most-photographed building in Alaska," the **Arctic**

## GOLD RUSH GHOSTS

Skagway is just the kind of place where you'd expect to see ghosts.

The most famous one is "Mary," who reputedly resides in Room 24 at the Golden North Hotel. Mary came to Skagway during the Klondike Gold Rush to wed her fiancé. Telling her to wait at the hotel, the young miner went off and was killed in the Palm Sunday avalanche on Chilkoot Pass. Refusing to believe he had died, Mary faithfully waited in her room, eventually dying of consumption. "She roams the halls in a long, white gown, sometimes in a veil, sometimes with her hair piled on her head," says the hotel owner.

The Red Onion also claims a ghost, described—usually by men—as "a hostile female presence." There's a whiff of perfume when the "presence" is present, and she's credited with locking doors, making pounding noises upstairs (where the brothel used to be), and watering plants in the owner's locked office.

The Eagles Hall has a ghost, too. This one's a blond, blue-eyed boy ghost. "Any officer who's been doing the books late at night has felt its presence," claims one local.

**Brotherhood Hall.** Built in 1899, the AB Hall was the headquarters of a now-defunct secret fraternal organization. The brotherhood was formed on board the steamship *City of Seattle* by 11 gold seekers. The Skagway group eventually numbered 300 and there were about 30 "camps" throughout Alaska and the Yukon, including Dawson City and Nome. The last person initiated into the Skagway camp was President Warren G. Harding in 1923.

The facade, considered a prime example of Victorian Rustic architecture, was made from 20,000 driftwood sticks collected on the tideflats. AB member Charles O. Walker is credited with creating the facade in 1900. From across the street you can see the driftwood letters "1899," "AB," and "Camp Skagway No. 1." The group's gold pan and nuggets insignia is up at the top.

The hall houses the **Trail of '98 Skagway Historical Museum and Archives.** The collection centers on Victorian life in Skagway, as well as the gold rush and Native culture. The archives contain historical materials and early governmental, business, and social organization records, plus photographs. Open 9 a.m.–5 p.m. daily mid-May to mid-September; by appointment during the winter. Admission is $2 for adults; $1 for children and students. For more information, call (907) 983-2420. 🚻 ♿

🚶 *Continue up the street to the corner of Third and Broadway.*

The 1900 building you pass on the way originally was the Alaska Steamship Co. office.

❺ On the southwest corner of Third and Broadway is the three-story **Golden North Hotel**, probably the oldest operating hotel in Alaska. This is Skagway's second Golden North Hotel. The original was located on Fourth Avenue, between State and Main Streets. The present hotel, with its distinctive domed turret, was built a block away on the corner of Third and State Streets in 1898 as the two-story Klondike Trading Company. In 1908, George Dedman and Edward Foreman, owners of the first Golden North, bought the building, remodeled it into a new Golden North, moved it, and added a third floor.

In the 1960s, different owners asked Skagway's pioneering gold rush families to donate furniture and other period mementos to furnish a room; in return, the room would be dedicated to that family. Room numbers were drawn from a hat and today guests can stay in rooms dedicated to the Dedman family, the Rapuzzis, the Pullens, and many other longtime Skagwayans. The hotel also is reputed to have a gold rush-era ghost. Note for movie buffs: The wolf dream scene in the movie *Never Cry Wolf* was shot at the Golden North in 1981.

Across Third, on Broadway, look for the Sweet Tooth Cafe. ✗ SWEET TOOTH CAFE

## WHO STRUCK IT RICH?

It's estimated that 40,000 men and women went off in search of gold in the Klondike. Of that number, it's further estimated that only 20,000 actually looked for gold, 4,000 found gold, less than 100 became wealthy, and only about 12 remained wealthy for life. Among the most successful of those who sought their fortune was Seattle's John Nordstrom, founder of the company known today as the Nordstrom Department Stores.

🚶 *Cross Broadway Street.*

**❻** **The Mascot Block**—the three buildings at Third and Broadway—is owned by the National Park Service. All three have been repainted their original colors. **The Mascot Saloon** (1898) was one of some 70 saloons then operating in Skagway. Now part of Klondike Gold Rush National Historical Park, the building houses an excellent exhibit of an old-time saloon. 🚻 ♿

Next door is the 1898 building that formerly housed the Pacific Clipper Line, one of several steamship companies that had their offices in this part of town, and the former Hern Liquor Store, built in 1937.

Other gold-rush era buildings in this block include the Skaguay (sic.) News Depot (1899), the Richter complex (three adjacent buildings constructed in 1899, 1929, and 1972), and the small building at the south end, now a liquor store but originally constructed in 1898 as the Hot Scotch Saloon. In the middle of the block is French Alley. The second building down the alley, now a gift shop, is a 1902 "crib," a small building used by early-day prostitutes.

🚶 *From the Mascot Block, proceed north on Broadway from Third to Fourth Avenue.*

Most of the buildings you'll pass on Broadway

between Third and Fourth were built at the turn of
the century, including the Lynch & Kennedy building (1900).

Across the street, in the center of the block, is
Dedman's Photo, built in 1897 as the studio for gold
rush photographer E.A. Hegg. George Dedman
arrived in 1898 with $16 and an iron in his suitcase.
A "lady of the evening" allowed him to launder a
pair of sheets, thus launching Dedman in the laundry business. He was one of the owners of the first
Golden North Hotel and later purchased the building that houses the present Golden North. His wife
established the photography business, which is still
run by members of their family.

**❼** On the corner of Fourth and Broadway is the
tallest building in Skagway, the three-story **Pack
Train Building**, constructed in 1904
as Army barracks and relocated from
a site two blocks up Broadway. The
corner business was a saloon called
The Trail (the big sign on the Fourth
Avenue side reading "U-AU-TO-NO-
THE-TRAIL" dates from that time).

🚶 *Continue on Broadway across Fourth Avenue.*

As you cross the street, look up on the bluff for the
**"Kirmses clock,"** a large timepiece painted on the
rock at the turn of the century. Originally commissioned by jeweler Peter Kern, it was later maintained by another jeweler, Herman Kirmse, and his
descendants.

**❽** Behind the Skagway Hardware
store (1900), is the historic **St.
James Hotel** (1898)—now used as
a warehouse. The saloon of this
hotel is where the deal was struck
in the spring of 1898 to build the
White Pass & Yukon Railroad. Local
lore has it that Sir Thomas Tancrede, representing

*Left:* Tiny "crib" once belonging to a Skagway lady of the evening now houses a gift shop. *Top:* The Skagway Street Car Company conducts tours in colorful, vintage national park touring cars. *Bottom:* The "Kirmses Clock" was painted on the bluff above Skagway around the turn of the century.

railroad investment interests in London, and Canadian Pacific Railway contractor Michael J. "Big Mike" Heney met by chance, talked through the night, and reached agreement by dawn.

🚶 *Return to Broadway, turn right to Fifth Avenue.*

Between Fourth and Fifth Avenues are buildings that date from the gold rush era, including:

- The Keelar the Money King Store (1900), two doors up from the hardware store. Frank Keelar was the self-described "Money King of Alaska," a wheeler-dealer who advertised that he "Loans Money—Buys Outfits," and claimed to own "mines, saw mills, steamboats, timber lands, and townsites" and to have "barrels of money."
- A 1901 prostitute's "crib," which is now a tiny gift shop.

🚶 *Turn left on Fifth and cross Broadway.*

❾ The **Skagway Visitors Bureau**, operated by the Skagway Convention and Visitors Bureau, is on Fifth just off Broadway; (907) 983-2855. Drop in and get the lowdown on what's happening and what to do in Skagway. 🚻 ♿

A short way beyond, at Fifth and State, is the Portland House Restaurant and Inn. 🚻 ♿ ✗ PORTLAND HOUSE RESTAURANT

🚶 *Retrace your steps back across Broadway and continue on Fifth about halfway down the block and cross the street.*

❿ On a large, grassy lot is the log **Moore Cabin**, built in 1887 as the residence of the founder of Skagway, Captain William "Billy" Moore. To the right is the house built in 1897 by Moore's son Bernard. To the left is the former Goldberg Cigar Store (1897). The National Park Service is restoring the buildings.

NPS archaeologists recently discovered that the lawn between the cabin and the cigar store is the beginning of the historic **White Pass Trail**, one of two routes used by the stampeders to reach the Klondike.

**🚶 *Retrace your steps back on Fifth Avenue to Broadway, turn right and continue to Sixth Avenue.***

Between Fifth and Sixth Avenues, you'll pass the Kirmse Jewelry Store (1899) and two other gold rush-era buildings.

**❶❶** On the southeast corner of Sixth and Broadway is **Eagles Hall**, venue for Skagway's "Days of '98" show, Alaska's longest running theatrical production, dating to 1927. The hall comprises two 1898 hotels, the Mondamin and the Pacific, placed end-to-end in 1920. The show, a Gay '90s melodrama featuring "Soapy Smith" and a re-creation of the historic shootout, as well as dance hall girls, can-can dancing,

and ragtime music, plays nightly during the summer season. Show times are posted at the theater, or call (907) 983-2545 for information.

Diagonally across from the Eagles Hall is the National Bank of Alaska Building, with the only ATM in Skagway. Next to the bank is the U.S. Post Office. Just past the Post Office, at 655 Broadway, is Lorna's, at the Skagway Inn. 🅢 ✉ 🍴 LORNA'S

**🚶 *Turn right on Sixth. As you near the end of the block, cross the street.***

**❶❷** **Mollie Walsh Park** is dedicated to a young woman who arrived alone in Skagway in the fall of 1897 and came to be known as "The Angel of White Pass" for her kindness to the miners at a "grub tent" she operated on the White Pass Trail.

*Left, top:* Certain Skagway was destined for big things, Captain Billy Moore built this cabin in 1887, a decade before the big gold rush. *Left, bottom:* A spurned suitor commissioned this bronze bust to memorialize Mollie Walsh, the "Angel of White Pass." *Above:* Fine dining and an historic inn combine at this popular Skagway establishment.

Numerous packers vied for her attentions, most notably "Packer Jack" Newman, who shot and killed a man in a fit of jealousy. After an argument with Newman about still another packer, Mollie married the other man, Mike Bartlett. The Bartletts eventually moved to Seattle, where Mike shot and killed Mollie in 1902 in a jealous rage. Newman was heartbroken when he learned of her death and in 1930, a year before his own death, he commissioned the bronze bust in this park. 🏙

Across from the park is the two-story former Peniel Mission (1900), now owned by the National Park Service.

🚶 *From the park, continue to the right, around the corner to an informational display about Pullen House.*

**⓭** Harriet "Ma" Pullen left a bankrupt farm in Washington state and hit Skagway in September 1897 with just $7 and a few possessions. Working in a tent restaurant, she baked pies from dried apples. Later she opened her own restaurant and rented out rooms in her three-story house, eventually buying the building and several others on the property. Her **Pullen House** became known as the finest hotel in the North. It operated for another decade after her death in 1947.

All that remains of the famous Pullen House is a tall stone chimney. The property is overgrown with trees and bushes, so it's not easy to photograph much of anything, including the chimney. (Please respect that the ruins are on private property and do not trespass.)

🚶 *From the Pullen House display, continue to the left along a dirt path, crossing a small footbridge over Pullen Creek.*

Depending on time of year, Dolly Varden trout as well as coho, pink, and chum salmon may be seen in the creek.

THEY CALL THE WIND . . . SKAGWAY

"Skagua" was the Tlingit name for the place. The name has various translations, most of which have something to do with wind. As Ben Moore, son of the city's founder, wrote: "Skagway is a name very typical of a place where the same air is never breathed twice."

Skagway takes a direct hit both from the bone-chilling winds that whistle off the mountains to the north and those that scream up Lynn Canal from the south. "The wind sounds like a freight train coming down the valley," said a local. "There are far more windy days than calm days. In fact, when it is calm, you know something's different as soon as you step outside—it's quiet." Another noted that in 1938 the wind was so strong it blew over the train cars of the White Pass & Yukon Route.

**14** The footpath leads to **Skagway's City Hall**. One of the few stone buildings in Alaska, it was constructed as a Methodist school, named McCabe College in honor of Bishop C.C. McCabe. The second-story Gothic-arch windows hint at its original purpose. As construction was under way, Congress passed legislation creating public schools in the Territory of Alaska and the Methodist school was no longer necessary. The U.S. District Court used it until 1956, when the city purchased it.

On the City Hall grounds is an **old WP&YR engine** and an interpretive display about steam locomotive #195, built in 1943 and barged to Skagway to alleviate a wartime locomotive shortage.

🚶 *From City Hall, go straight ahead (west) on Seventh Avenue to Broadway.*

OPTION A: To conclude your walking tour, turn left and return back on Broadway five blocks to your starting point.

OPTION B: Continue the walking tour by crossing Broadway and proceeding on Seventh another block to State Street and turn right for the half-hour to 45-minute walk to the Gold Rush Cemetery.

OPTION C: Pass up the walk to the Gold Rush Cemetery. Cross Broadway, turn right on State Street to Eighth Avenue, turn left, and proceed one block to Main Street (skip to Stop #16).

---

🚶 *Go past Broadway to State Street. Turn right and walk 16 blocks to 23rd Avenue. Continue to the left on 23rd for about two blocks.*

You'll pass the WP&YR yards on the right. Brown and white park service signs point the way to the cemetery. (You may be tempted to take a shortcut through the WP&YR yard, but this is private property and you could be cited for trespassing.)

🚶 *Turn right off the main highway onto a dirt road that loops around the WP&YR yards. Follow the dirt road across the railroad tracks and continue about 0.4 mile (10 more minutes) to the cemetery on the right.*

**15** From Seventh and State, it's about 1½ miles on level, mostly paved, sidewalk or street to the **Gold Rush Cemetery**. The boardwalks of Skagway's historic district give way to concrete sidewalks and you'll pass through a mostly contemporary residential area.

Jefferson R. Smith

Died July 8-1898

Aged 38 Years

On State Street you may see ore trucks with huge "pots" on the trailers, hauling lead and zinc ore from Faro, Yukon Territory, to the huge brown terminal—the "biggest little ore house"—at Skagway's harbor.

This was Skagway's city cemetery during the gold rush and dozens of pioneers and stampeders are buried here. The cemetery was used from 1897 until 1908, when another site was developed across the Skagway River. Among the notable Skagwayans buried here are Frank Reid and Jefferson Randolph "Soapy" Smith, who killed each other during a shoot-out in 1898. There's a path up the hill a short way to 300-foot-high Reid Falls.

You'll also see "the world's biggest gold nugget," a gold-painted boulder chained near the grave of Martin Itjen, an Austrian immigrant who was Skagway's first tourism promoter. Itjen was one of Skagway's early day characters; his Skagway Street Car Company conducted tours that included the cemetery. (The streetcar company has been revived by a local couple, who operate antique national park sightseeing cars and a theater complex downtown.)

🚶‍♂️🚶 *Retrace your route back to town along the dirt road, 23rd Avenue and State Street to Eighth Avenue. Turn right on Eighth and proceed one block to Main Street.*

On the way, you'll pass by the **Skagway Public Library** on the southwest corner of Eighth and State.

**16** At Eighth and Main, is the "plantation-style" **White House**, built in 1902 as the home of saloon owner Lee Guthrie. Later the house was used as a hotel and was an Army hospital during World War II. It's now a bed-and-breakfast.

🚶‍♂️🚶 *Turn left on Main Street for one block, then turn right on Seventh Avenue for another block.*

**17** Two historic houses are near the corner of Seventh Avenue and Alaska Street, on the righthand side of the street.

The first you'll come to is the **Nye House**, which originated as a log cabin during the gold rush. Additions were made to it from 1898 to 1901. The house

was the long-time residence of Charley Nye, a power company executive.

The second house is the **Case-Mulvihill House**, a Victorian-style residence dating from 1904, when it was the home of W.H. Case, a partner in the noted photographic company of Case and Draper, who made many historic photographs during the gold rush. About 10 years later, William J. Mulvihill, chief dispatcher for the WP&YR, moved in with his family. (Mulvihill also was elected mayor of Skagway an astonishing 16 times.)

🚶 *At the corner of Seventh Avenue and Alaska Street, turn left for one block to Sixth Avenue, and turn left.*

**18** On the southeast corner is the **Gault House** (1899). This building may have originated as a saloon when Sixth Avenue was Skagway's primary business street. (The city was later re-oriented north and south and Broadway became the main business center.) For many years it was the home of Roy Gault, a WP&YR engineer.

🚶 *Continue on Sixth Avenue one block to Main Street and turn right one block.*

**19** Skagway's only remaining gold rush-era church is the **First Presbyterian Church**, on the southwest corner of Fifth Avenue and Main Street. The Methodists built it in 1901 after they sold McCabe College to the U.S. government. In 1917, a Presbyterian congregation bought it.

🚶 *Continue down Main Street four blocks to First Avenue.*

**20** At the northwest corner of First and Main are three **houses built by the WP&YR** for its employees after the gold rush.

🚶 *From here you have two alternatives:*

---

OPTION A:

🚶 *Turn right on First Avenue and follow the street and then a footpath past the end of the airport's runway (it's fenced off for your safety—so don't climb over) to a suspension bridge (built in 1994) over the Skagway River.*

㉑ On the other side of the footbridge is the trailhead for a 0.4-mile hike to **Yakutania Point**. It's well-marked and there are exercise stations along the way.

Return from the hike and follow Option B, below.

---

OPTION B:

🚶 *Turn left on First Avenue and return to Broadway Street and the dock area.*

㉒ On the way, you'll pass a row of **mountain ash trees** planted along First Avenue. Plaques at the trees memorialize pioneer Skagway and Dyea families.

At First and State, you'll also pass the rather undistinguished-looking marker for the location of the **Frank Reid-Soapy Smith shootout**.

---

🚶 *At Broadway, turn left to return to the National Park Service visitor center and the main shopping district, or right to the ferry terminal and cruise ship piers.*

*Left, top:* One of the more than 500 curves along the rail bed of the White Pass & Yukon Route. *Left, bottom:* Up to 3,000 intrepid hikers tackle the rugged Chilkoot Trail each summer. *Above:* White Pass & Yukon Route narrow-gauge train emerges from the 250-foot tunnel that was blasted through solid rock.

# Getting Out of Town

## TAKE A HIKE: DEWEY LAKES TRAIL

The Dewey Lakes trail system is Skagway's most accessible. To reach the trailhead, walk east on Fourth Avenue toward the bluff, cross the footbridge over Pullen Creek, and look for the sign on the other side of the railroad tracks.

It's a fairly easy, half-hour hike for slightly more than half a mile to Lower Dewey Lake. The hike offers good views of Skagway. Upper Dewey Lake is approximately 2.5 miles beyond the lower lake, up a steep, strenuous, switchback trail.

Obtain Skagway-area trail maps at the Visitor Information Center, on Fifth just off Broadway, or the National Park Service visitor center, Second and Broadway.

## WP&YR: RAILWAY BUILT OF GOLD

Alaska's first railroad, the White Pass & Yukon Route, was pushed through the rugged Coastal Mountain Range at the turn of the century to provide stampeders easier access to the Klondike.

Construction of the 110-mile narrow-gauge railroad up White Pass from Skagway to Whitehorse, Yukon Territory, was an incredible engineering feat for its time. Completed in an astonishing 26 months, the railroad negotiates more than 500 curves along a roadbed hand-carved from sheer rock cliffs and passes through a 250-foot tunnel blasted through the rock. It climbs 2,885 feet from sea level in its first 21 miles. A major accomplishment in 1901 was the construction of a steel cantilever bridge arching 215 feet above Cutoff Canyon, at one time the highest railroad bridge in the world. The bridge has been replaced by a newer span, but the old one can be seen today from the passing train—particularly eerie on a foggy day when it looks like a ghost bridge to nowhere.

The railroad is designated an International Historic Civil Engineering Landmark. Excursions to the summit aboard the gold-rush era rail cars are sold on board cruise ships or at the WP&YR station. Call (907) 983-2217 or (800) 343-7373 for information.

## CHILKOOT TRAIL:
## WORLD'S LONGEST MUSEUM

The 33-mile Chilkoot Trail was one of the major routes to the Klondike, and one of the most grueling. The last 4 miles—known as the Golden Stairs—is a strenuous 45-degree climb. During March and April of 1898, 1,200 to 1,500 steps carved in the ice provided access; some of the most famous photographs of the gold rush were taken here documenting the column of men and women struggling up the steep grade. Hazards abounded. The Palm Sunday avalanche on April 3, 1898, killed some 70 stampeders, many of whom are buried in the Slide Cemetery near the ghost town of Dyea. Today, the Chilkoot is known as the "world's longest museum," for the thousands of artifacts from the gold rush that line the trail (please do not touch or remove any artifact). About 2,500 to 3,000 hikers brave the trail each summer.

The route is just as rugged as ever. The weather can be cold and wet; you may have to hike through snow, even in July. A trail permit is required and you must pre-clear Canadian customs before you go. The trail is part of Klondike Gold Rush National Historical Park. For information, check with the NPS park visitor center at Second and Broadway, (907) 983-2921.

### HOP OVER TO HAINES

Haines is just 15 miles by water down Lynn Canal from Skagway (360 miles if you drive), making it an easy day trip.

The Chilkat Bald Eagle Preserve near Haines is one of the best places in the world to see bald eagles. They flock to the Chilkat River each fall to feed on a late run of spawning salmon. The American Bald Eagle Foundation has an interpretive museum in Haines; free admission.

Other attractions are Fort William H. Seward, a National Historic Landmark, which offers a salmon bake and performances by the Chilkat Dancers; the Sheldon Museum and Cultural Center; and a re-created 1890s gold rush city.

An easy way to get to Haines is via the Haines-Skagway Water Taxi, (907) 766-3395. Fares are $29 round-trip; $18 one way.

# Sitka at a Glance

**Population:**   City and Borough of Sitka: 8,632 (20.9.5% Alaska Natives); 52% Men; 48% Women; Visitors: 200,000 annually

**Geography:**   City and Borough of Sitka: 2,881.5 sq. mi. Location: Sitka Sound, on the west coast of Baranof Island, 95 air miles southwest of Juneau, 185 air miles northwest of Ketchikan, and 862 miles northwest of Seattle

**Weather:**   Average summer temperatures: 48–61° F Average winter temperatures: 23–35° F Annual precipitation: 95" Solstices: Summer (June 21): almost 18 hours of daylight. Winter (Dec. 21): 6 hours, 41 minutes of daylight

**Primary Industries:**   Fishing and fish processing; also, tourism (300 cruise ship calls each summer), retail, government, transportation, health services

**Facilities and Services:**   Sheldon Jackson College and a branch of the University of Alaska Southeast; Sitka Community Hospital and Mt. Edgecumbe Hospital (a regional medical center); 21 churches. Newspaper: *Daily Sitka Sentinel*. TV: Cable channels. Radio: KCAW-FM 104.7; KIFW-AM 1230; KSBZ-FM 103.1

**Visitor Information:**   Centennial Building Visitors Information, 330 Harbor Drive, (907) 747-3225. What to do in Sitka and surrounding area. Sitka National Historical Park Visitors Center, 106 Metlakatla St., (907) 747-6281. The nation's smallest national park. Sitka Ranger District, Tongass National Forest, 201 Katlian St., Suite 109, (907) 747-6671. Forest Service cabins and hikes.

# Sitka

*Old records reveal that the Russians grumbled about the rain when* **they** *were in the Sitka area, too.*

S itka-by-the-Sea is a sparkling jewel in the necklace of port cities along the fabled Inside Passage. Its distinct personality is forged from its Tlingit Indian roots and flavored by the Russian influence of the eighteenth and nineteenth centuries. Sitka pays homage to both cultures in restored Russian buildings and historic sites as well as a totem park and Native arts and crafts center. Downtown's major street diverges around Sitka's majestic centerpiece, St. Michael's Russian Orthodox Cathedral. When you walk through this charming town, you follow the still-echoing footsteps of an earlier era.

With a population of nearly 9,000 and its location on the Pacific Ocean side of Baranof Island, Sitka has the small-town flavor (it got its first traffic light in 1992) and wilderness accessibility so prevalent in Southeast Alaska. It also hosts such cultural events as the Sitka Summer Music Festival, featuring world-renowned classical musicians; a writers symposium; and Sitka Fine Arts Camp for Youth. Two colleges lend their influence to the local milieu. But regardless of how high-falutin' the activity, Sitkans take it all in stride. A local noted that even for the music festival, "you can dress up or go in your XtraTufs (rubber boots)."

With mountains at its back and the Pacific at its doorstep, Sitka has a spectacular setting. And its island life creates its own style. Garage sale-ing is very big, although as one local laughed: "Here we are on this rock and everything's just recycling from one house to another." A few independent folks prefer their own islands, residing on one of the dozen or so private islands in Sitka Sound and commuting via power or rowboat.

*"If you want to get really wild, you have to go out of town—go to Juneau."*

This scenic site on Sitka Sound was occupied for hundreds of years by the Kiksadi Clan of Tlingits, who had four longhouses on what is now Castle Hill. The village was Shee-Atika, meaning "people on the outside of Shee (Baranof Island)." Shee-Atika provided a good life; the Tlingits harvested fish from the ocean, hunted deer and bear, and gathered berries. Their 60-foot-long cedar canoes journeyed north to the Copper River on the Gulf of Alaska and south to what is now Oregon and northern California.

The year 1741 tolled the beginning of the end for this idyll. Vitus Bering, a Danish navigator in the service of the Russian czar, sailed east from Siberia's Kamchatka Peninsula. Those explorations led to the Russian colonization of Alaska, spurred by the hunt for sea otter pelts. Within a few years, 43 fur-trading companies were operating in Alaska; eventually the Russian empire extended from Fort Ross, near San Francisco, to the Aleutian Islands and even farther up the coast of the Bering Sea.

*One local laughed about Sitka's penchant for garage sales: "Here we are on this rock and everything's just recycling from one house to another."*

In 1799, Alexander Baranov, manager of the Russian-American Company, arrived at Shee-Atika. Wary of the Tlingits, Baranov built an outpost, Fort Archangel Saint Michael, at what is now called Old Sitka, 7 miles from downtown. The Kiksadis were equally wary of the Russians, and in 1802, Chief Katlian and his warriors destroyed the fort. Baranov returned two years later with four ships and a contingent of Aleut warriors. The Kiksadis had moved to a fortified compound called Shish-Kee-Nu, near the mouth of the Indian River. The Russian ships opened fire, but the Tlingits remained quiet. A Russian landing party was launched, and when it drew near, Chief Katlian led a charge, wearing his Raven hat and brandishing a blacksmith's hammer acquired in the 1802 raid. The Russian and Aleut forces beat a retreat.

*"We have an inordinate amount of wildlife—a dozen or more whales spouting at any one time."*

Six days of negotiations and bombardment continued, to no avail. During that time, the Tlingits' ammunition was inadvertently destroyed, leaving them in an untenable position. At dawn on October 7, the Tlingit fort was eerily quiet. The Tlingits had slipped away in the night; the Battle of Alaska was over.

The Russians burned the compound and established a settlement called New Archangel, which became their new capital. During the 1800s it was the largest, most sophisticated city on the west coast of North America, hailed as the "Paris of the Pacific."

The Russian era concluded in 1867, with the United States' purchase of Russian America. New Archangel became Sitka and continued as the seat of government until 1906, when Juneau became the capital.

A spate of gold mining, Sheldon Jackson Institute, and the fishing industry sustained Sitka's economy. During World War II, the town was fortified and the U.S. Navy built an air base on Japonski Island, which

later became Mount Edgecumbe School, a boarding school for Alaska Native children. A large pulp mill operated from 1959 until 1993. As Sitka approaches its bicentennial, its economy depends on fishing, fish processing, tourism, retail, government, transportation, and health services.

Sitka's active arts community features several dance groups; numerous art galleries; two museums; and

*Left:* View of the Pioneers' Home and Sitka's western waterfront from Japonski Island. *Above:* Dramatic view of St. Michael's Russian Orthodox Cathedral.

theater, music and choral groups. Sport fishing for salmon and halibut is popular, as are bird- and whale-watching.

There are miles of trails and pathways for bicycling and walking or running.

### FESTIVALS AND OTHER FUN

Special Sitka events include: A two-week Mother's Day Quilt Show in May; Sitka Salmon Derby on Memorial Day weekend; in June, the three-week Sitka Summer Music Festival, the Sitka Symposium on Human Values and the Written Word, and the Sitka Fine Arts Camp for Youth; the Running of the Boots, late summer, with a "boot race" and prizes for the ugliest, biggest, etc. boots; Alaska Day Festival, with a week of events leading up to the October 18 reenactment of the transfer of Alaska to the United States; and the Sitka WhaleFest in November, with whale watching, photography workshops, art displays, and more.

### DON'T MISS

- The Alaska Raptor Rehabilitation Center (Stop #6 on the walking tour), where you can make the acquaintance of a bald eagle and other birds of prey.
- Sitka National Historical Park (Stop #7), to learn about Sitka's past and see Native artworks being created.
- The Russian Bishop's House (Stop #2), built for a prelate who held sway over an area extending from San Francisco to Japan.
- The views from Castle Hill (Stop #20), the best spot to photograph downtown, Sitka Sound, and all around.
- St. Michael's Russian Orthodox Cathedral (Stop #11), with its priceless icons and other treasures.

### GRABBING A BITE

Following are a few suggested dining spots. The number indicates where to look for them as you follow the walking tour.

- The Bayview Restaurant, upstairs in the MacDonald Bayview Trading Company, 407 Lincoln St. (between Stops #1 and #2). Gourmet burgers, deli sandwiches, soups, espresso, Russian specialties. Wine and beer. Open daily in the summer. $–$$

- The Raven Room, in the Westmark Shee Atika Hotel, 330 Seward St. (between Stops #10 and #11). Features local seafood, including Dungeness crab and beer-battered halibut. Full bar. Daily breakfast, lunch, dinner. $$$

- The Backdoor Cafe, 104 Barracks St. (in the back of Old Harbor Books; Stop #13). Sandwiches, pastries, espresso. Sooner or later, you'll meet everyone in town here. $

- Marina Restaurant, 205 Harbor Drive (5 minutes west of the Centennial Bldg.; Stop #1). Try the pizza and pasta. Full bar. Daily lunch and dinner. Closed Sundays in January and February. $$

- Van Winkle and Daigler Frontier Cuisine, 228 Harbor Drive (5 minutes west of the Centennial Bldg.; Stop #1). Classic Alaska atmosphere. Try the mud pie. Full bar. Daily lunch and dinner; breakfast on Sundays. $$

## STOP TO SHOP

Numerous shops are along Lincoln Street, offering everything from Native art to specialty teas. A few suggested places to shop:

- Sitka Rose Gallery, 419 Lincoln St. Sculpture, painting, and Native art of more than 80 artisans from across Alaska, including Tlingit co-owner and artist Teri Rofkar.

- The Russian American Company, upstairs in the Mac-Donald Bayview Trading Company, 407 Lincoln St. Russian lacquer boxes, icons, and matrioshka (nesting) dolls.

- Old Harbor Books, 201 Lincoln St. New and used books (a large collection of Alaska books), nautical charts, maps, greeting cards.

- Fairweather Prints, 209 Lincoln St. Hand-painted designer dresses and tops; original T-shirts and sweatshirts. Silk scarves, jewelry, and gifts.

- Chocolate Moose, 120 Lincoln St. Fine chocolates, specialty teas and coffees, Sitka Sweets wild berry candies, espresso drinks.

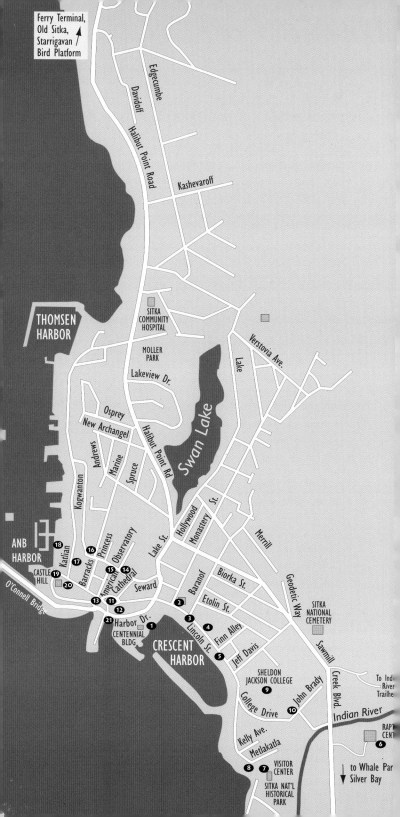

Ferry Terminal,
Old Sitka,
Starrigavan
Bird Platform

Edgecumbe

Davidoff

Halibut Point Road

Kashevaroff

Verstovia Ave.

Lake

THOMSEN
HARBOR

SITKA
COMMUNITY
HOSPITAL

MOLLER
PARK

Lakeview Dr.

Osprey

New Archangel

Andrews

Marine

Spruce

Halibut Point Rd

Swan Lake

Kogwanton

Katlian

Barracks

Princess

Observatory

American

Cathedral

Seward

Lake St.

Hollywood

Monastery St.

Merrill

Baranof

Biorka St.

Etolin St.

Geodetic Way

SITKA
NATIONAL
CEMETERY

ANB
HARBOR

CASTLE
HILL

O'Connell Bridge

Harbor Dr.

CENTENNIAL
BLDG

Lincoln St.

Finn Alley

Jeff Davis

Sawmill

Creek Blvd.

To Ind
River
Trailhe

CRESCENT
HARBOR

SHELDON
JACKSON COLLEGE

College Drive

John Brady

Indian River

RAP
CEN

Kelly Ave.

Metlakatla

VISITOR
CENTER

SITKA NAT'L
HISTORICAL
PARK

to Whale Par
Silver Bay

18  17  16  15  14  13  11  12  21  19  20  1  2  3  4  5  9  10  6  7  8

# The Walking Tour

# Sitka Walking Tour

This walking tour takes you through Sitka's mostly level downtown. You'll see historic Russian buildings and a Native cultural center, learn about local and Native history at Sitka National Historical Park and the Sheldon Jackson Museum, and have the option of seeing bald eagles face-to-face at the Alaska Raptor Rehabilitation Center. The tour takes 2 to 2½ hours or more, depending on how long you linger at museums and shops. The walk to the Raptor Center adds at least another hour.

❶ The walking tour starts on the waterfront at the **Centennial Building Visitors Center**, 330 Harbor Drive.

🚶 *If you're arriving at the cruise ship dock, it's to your left. If you're coming from the ferry terminal, head into town on Halibut Point Road, turn right on Lake Street, which curves to the right to become Harbor Drive. The Centennial Building is to the left in the curve.*

The **Centennial Building** was dedicated on Seward's Day, March 30, 1967, as part of the centennial of the United States purchase of Alaska from Russia. On the grounds is a large Tlingit canoe, hand-hewn from a single log. The building's brass doorpulls copy Haida Indian argillite carvings of Raven and Bear. Find out

what to see and do in and around Sitka at the information desk; (907) 747-3225. 🚻 ♿

The Centennial Building also houses the **Isabel Miller Museum**; (907) 747-6459. Operated by the Sitka Historical Society, it has a scale model of the downtown area as it looked on the date of transfer from Russia to the United States, and a Victorian parlor complete with "windows" that look into dioramas of the town. Tlin-

## THE NEW ARCHANGEL DANCERS

Sitka's New Archangel Dancers, a troupe of about 35 women, performs traditional Russian, Byelo-Russian, Moladavian, Ukranian, Georgian, and Armenian folk dances. The performances are professionally choreographed and feature authentic costumes.

The group was formed in 1969 to promote Sitka's Russian history. Men were invited to join back then, but none would. Now, they're not allowed. (Sorry, guys.) The women perform all the roles, even the male roles requiring great strength and endurance.

The all-volunteer, nonprofit group travels all over the United States, as well as Russia and other European countries. Well over a million people have seen their performances. During the summer, they perform up to five shows a day at the Centennial Building on Sitka's central waterfront.

Admission is $6 per person. A schedule is posted in the building, or you can call (907) 747-3225 for show times. The New Archangel Dancers performance is included on city tours sold aboard many cruise ships or from Sitka Tours, (907) 747-8443.

git artifacts, a copy of the U.S. Treasury warrant used to buy Alaska, and Russian Orthodox icons also are displayed. Open daily, 8 a.m.–6 p.m. during the summer season; Mon.–Fri., 10 a.m.–5 p.m. the rest of the year. Special hours accommodate ferry stopovers. Admission is free ($1 donation is asked). There is a small gift shop.

This is also the summer home for the New Archangel Dancers, a world-renowned troupe of women who perform traditional Russian folk dances. Call (907) 747-3225 for show times.

About 5 minutes west of the Centennial Building are Marina Restaurant, (205 Harbor Drive) and Van Winkle and Daigler Frontier Cuisine (228 Harbor Drive). ✕ MARINA RESTAURANT; VAN WINKLE AND DAIGLER FRONTIER CUISINE

🚶 *From the Centennial Building, walk out to Harbor Drive, and go right for about a block. Harbor Drive becomes Lake Street. Cross Lincoln Street and turn right (east) after one block to Monastery Street.*

*Left, top:* The Russian Bishop's House originally was completed in 1843; renovations by the National Park Service were finished in 1988. *Left, bottom:* Sitka's New Archangel Dancers have performed around the world. *Above:* The oldest grave in Sitka National Cemetery dates from 1867.

There are a postal substation and restrooms at MacDonald's Bayview Trading Co., at 407 Lincoln Street. The Bayview Restaurant is upstairs. There's an ATM at First Bank, 208C Lake Street. ✉ 🏧 💲

✕ BAYVIEW RESTAURANT

Lincoln Street follows the "Governor's Walk," so named because the Russian governor, Alexander Baranov, is said to have often walked here. A park along Lincoln Street borders **Crescent Harbor**, one of Sitka's four small boat harbors. As you cross Monastery, look to your left for a Southeast Alaska oddity—a tree growing on top of a utility pole about half a block up Monastery on the righthand side.

**②** On the corner of Lincoln and Monastery is the **Russian Bishop's House and Museum**, one of only four intact Russian buildings in North America. Com-

pleted in 1843, the house was first occupied by Father Ivan Veni-aminov—Bishop Innocent—whose diocese stretched from 60 miles north of San Francisco to 30 miles north of Hokkaido, Japan. The clergyman, teacher, physician, and scientist spent 16 years at Sitka. His dedication earned him the highest ecclesiastical post in Russian Orthodoxy: Metropolitan of Moscow.

The two-story building was built by Finnish shipwrights of logs with plank siding. The bishop's quarters and magnificent Chapel of the Annunciation are on the second floor, a school and orphanage were on the first floor. In 1969, the church closed the building because it was in danger of collapsing. After the National Park Service acquired the building in 1972 it began a 16-year project to meticulously restore the building to its 1853 appearance.

Open daily, 8:30 a.m.–4:30 p.m. during the summer. Times of free, guided tours are posted. Winter hours by appointment. Call (907) 747-6281.

The small building next to the Bishop's House was built c.1897 by the Orthodox Church and used as a school. In 1923, it became Sitka's first public library.

🚶 *Continue east on Lincoln Street one block to Baranof Street, the boundary of New Archangel in Russian times.*

❸ On the northeast corner of Lincoln and Baranof Streets is the **Emmons House**, built in 1895 by U.S. Navy Lt. George Thornton Emmons, an explorer who wrote about the early history of the Tlingits for the Museum of Natural History in New York and became a leading Alaska anthropologist.

🚶 *Continue east along Lincoln Street for about half a block.*

❹ At 611 Lincoln Street, Gothic-style **St. Peter's-by-the-Sea Episcopal Church** (one of the few stone buildings in Alaska) was built in 1899 under the auspices of Bishop Peter Trimble Rowe, Episcopal Bishop of Alaska. The congregation waited two years for their stained glass rose window. After it was installed, a concerned parishioner pointed out to Rowe that they had probably received another church's window, since the small center design was a Star of David. Rowe reportedly shushed the parishioner, admonishing "Don't say anything. They'll never notice."

Rowe and members of his family are buried in the front yard of the church. Behind the church is the See House, designed and built by the bishop in 1905, which houses church offices and a fellowship hall.

🚶 *From St. Peter's, continue east on Lincoln.*

On the left, you'll pass the Moore House, built in 1899; its history is posted on the fence. Across the street, the harbor park continues. Pavilions shelter benches and picnic tables.

🚶 *Cross Lincoln and walk along the park for a short way.*

❺ Just before the park's tennis courts, there's a large flat rock—about 2 feet high and 5 feet long—

---

### THE "ERUPTION" OF MOUNT EDGECUMBE

Rising 3,271 feet out of the Pacific Ocean about 15 miles west of Sitka, Mount Edgecumbe is one of the area's most eye-catching features. Beautiful and Fuji-like, the extinct volcano sat quietly for centuries. Then on April 1, 1974, Oliver J. "Porky" Bickar, a member of Sitka's practical-joke-playing "Dirty Dozen," set about staging an "eruption."

"I got a hundred or so tires together," Porky recalled. "I woke up April Fool's Day and you could see the mountain so clear. You could see a thousand miles. I said, 'I'm gonna do it.'"

Porky began dialing for pilots. "I finally got ahold of Earl Walker, with Temsco in Petersburg over on the other side of the island. He was sitting there all fogged in. And he said 'If I can see one more telephone pole, I'll come over.' And about an hour later, here he comes."

The pair flew over to the volcano with half the tires, plus some oily rags, gasoline, and a few smoke bombs for good measure. "I placed them in the middle of the crater. Then I stomped 40- or 50-foot-long letters in the snow saying 'April Fools!'" Porky added black paint to highlight the letters. Earl returned with the rest of the tires, and they set the whole mess on fire.

"We flew back real low and inconspicuous like," Porky chortled.

Black smoke billowed from Mount Edgecumbe's cone. The Coast Guard got all excited. Someone called an admiral and an aircraft flew for a look. Then came the radio message: "Looks like you've been had."

---

known today as **"Sitka's Blarney Stone."** The "blarney" connection is unclear—possibly from an early-day promoter. But there are two other stories about this particular rock. One says it was "Baranov's Rock," because Russian Governor Baranov used to rest on it during his constitutionals. According to earlier lore, the Tlingits called it "the Whetstone," because a long-ago chief sharpened his knives on it.

A short way farther, across from Sheldon Jackson College, is a larger rock with trees growing on it and a bronze plaque dedicated to Sheldon Jackson. The Tlingit legend referred to it as the "Grindstone" because the same chief used to grind the heads of his

SITKA

enemies on this rock. **Petroglyphs** on the rock are symbols carved most likely by ancestors of the region's Native peoples 2,000 to 8,000 years ago. Please respect these ancient antiquities by only photographing them.

🚶 *Cross Lincoln again to Jeff Davis Street.*

Sitka is perhaps the only place in the world where Jeff Davis and Lincoln Streets intersect. But this Davis was not the head of the Confederacy. General Jefferson C. Davis was a Union officer who fought under General Howard in the Civil War and became the first governor of Alaska after the transfer in 1867.

🚶 *Continue east on Lincoln past the Sheldon Jackson College Campus for 5 to 10 minutes to Sitka National Historical Park, skip to Stop #7, or take the optional route.*

OPTION: This optional route will take you to the **Alaska Raptor Rehabilitation Center**, 1011 Sawmill Creek Road, and into **Sitka National Historical Park** the back way. It's about 20 minutes to the Raptor Center and another 15 to 20 minutes to the park visitor center, but the whole detour can take an hour or more, depending on how long you visit the Raptor Center.

🚶 *From Lincoln Street, walk up Jeff Davis Street about four blocks to Sawmill Creek Boulevard, turn right, and follow the walkway/bike path on the right side of the road.*

### PIE IN THE SKY

If you fly into, or out of, Sitka, be sure to drop by the Nugget Restaurant in the airport terminal for a slice of their renowned pie—they'll pack it "to go." Southeasterners in the know do just that on Sitka stopovers, returning to the plane with their boxes of fruit-filled or cream pie. There's just enough time to savor a slice of "pie in the sky" before the plane gets to Juneau.

Across the highway is **Sitka National Cemetery**, one of the smallest national cemeteries in the United States. The oldest burial was in 1867. Just past the cemetery is the **Alaska Public Safety Academy**, where Alaska State Troopers are trained.

Look for the Raptor Center sign across the highway after the bridge over Indian River.

🚶 *Cross the highway, but be careful. There's no stoplight and traffic on Sawmill Creek Boulevard can be heavy. Walk the road up the hill for about 5 minutes to the Raptor Center.*

❻ The **Alaska Raptor Rehabilitation Center**, founded in 1980, is Alaska's primary facility for injured birds—from hummingbirds to bald eagles. The center treats about 200 birds each year, most  injured through interaction with humans. After rehabilitation, the birds are released. Non-releasable eagles, owls, and other raptors are placed in breeding programs or become educational birds. You may be greeted by Volta, a bald eagle that was injured in a collision with a power line; Hoot, a barred owl; or Gandalf, a great horned owl. Photographs are permitted. ARRC is a nonprofit, volunteer-operated facility, with a bird clinic, classrooms, auditorium, and gift shop.

Open 8 a.m.–5 p.m., mid-May to Sept. 30, when cruise ships are in port. There is a (tax-deductible) admission charge for the summer program. Winter hours are 8 a.m.–5 p.m., Mon.–Fri.; no formal program. Call (907) 747-8662 for information or to confirm hours.

🚶 *Go back down the hill and cross the highway. Continue to the left on the pathway for another 10 minutes to the park entrance, marked by park service signs. Follow the trail through the forested park for about 10 minutes, crossing Indian River, to the visitors center.*

**7** **Sitka National Historical Park** is Alaska's oldest and smallest national park, located on land set aside in 1890. It became a national historical park in 1972 and encompasses several sites significant in Sitka's Tlingit and Russian history, including the site of the Kiksadi Tlingit fort, Shish-Kee-Nu; the 1804 battleground; the Russian Bishop's House; and the Russian blockhouse

downtown. The center has an excellent exhibit of Alaska Native artifacts, including tools, baskets, jewelry, Tlingit house fronts, and house posts. A 10-minute slide program on the famous battle is shown in the auditorium.

One wing is devoted to the **Southeast Alaska Indian Cultural Center**, which provides instruction in traditional arts and crafts. In the summer, there is usually at least one artisan at work from 8 a.m. to 5 p.m.

A one-mile trail is lined with 11 totem poles, many carved in the 1930s as replicas of poles collected by Governor John Brady at the turn of the century and displayed at the St. Louis and Portland Expositions. The trail loops around the Kiksadi fort site. Rangers conduct guided walks; check at the visitors center for times.

Open daily, 8 a.m.–5 p.m., June–Sept.; 8 a.m.–5 p.m., Mon.–Fri., Oct.–May. The trail and park grounds are open 6 a.m.–10 p.m. in the summer; winter hours are shorter. No admission fee. For more information, call the park headquarters, (907) 747-6281. 🏛 ♿

From the visitors center, head out to Metlakatla Street, turn left back to town. Metlakatla turns into Lincoln Street at the corner.

**8** Near the corner, to the left, a stairway leads down a short way to a scenic viewpoint and **Merrill**

**Rock**. A plaque is dedicated to Elbridge W. Merrill, a photographer and the first custodian of the park, who lived in Sitka for more than 30 years. 📷

🥾 *Return to Lincoln Street and continue left 5 to 10 minutes.*

On the left, you'll pass the brown-and-cream building housing the **Sheldon Jackson Hatchery**, the only production hatchery on a college campus in the United States.

🥾 *Cross Lincoln and walk up College Drive to the campus.*

**9** Arranged around a broad lawn are the buildings of **Sheldon Jackson College**. In 1879, a Presbyterian missionary, the Rev. Alonzo Austin, founded an "industrial training school" that he named in 1881 for the famous Alaskan missionary and educator, the Rev. Dr. Sheldon Jackson. After an earlier building burned in 1882, Austin and his wife Isabelle established Sheldon Jackson Institute on its present site. The boarding school provided Native boys—and later girls—an eighth-grade education and training in skills such as carpentry and home economics. The present campus was built in 1911. The oldest educational institution in Alaska, Sheldon Jackson became a high school in 1917, a junior college in 1944, and a four-year college in 1976. It remains affiliated with the Presbyterian Church. Some 250–300 students—Native and non-Native—attend the school.

🥾 *Continue on College Drive toward the right to a large octagonal building.*

**10** **Sheldon Jackson Museum**, 104 College Drive, was the first concrete building in Alaska. As the first general agent of education for Alaska, the Rev. Dr. Sheldon Jackson traveled throughout the territory and acquired an extensive collection of Indian, Eskimo, and Aleut artifacts. In 1890, he built a museum for his collection. By 1895, the first museum was too small and the concrete structure was built. In 1984, it became part of the state museum system.

The building provides a circular setting for the cases—original to the museum—displaying an excellent collection of artifacts, most pre-dating the 1930s and many collected by Jack-son from 1888 to 1898. Tall cases line the perimeter, while cases of drawers are in the center. (Each drawer is a small adventure. You'll find ivory carvings, beadwork, and fishing gear, among other intriguing items.) The collection represents Alaska's four major Native groups: Eskimo, Athabaskan, Aleut, and Northwest Coast (including Tlingit, Haida, and Tsimshian).

Open daily 8 a.m.–5 p.m., mid-May to mid-Sept.; 10 a.m.–4 p.m. Tues.–Sat., mid-Sept. to mid-May. Admission: $3 for adults; children 18 and under—and students with valid ID cards—free. Free admission on Saturdays during the winter. Volunteers and staff are on hand to answer questions. A gift shop features Alaska Native handicrafts. 🚻 ♿

🚶 *From the museum, walk back down College Drive to Lincoln Street, turn right and proceed the five blocks back to Lake Street. Cross Lake Street and continue on Lincoln to the cathedral.*

Just up Lake Street, on the lefthand side, is the back entrance to the Westmark Shee Atika Hotel and the Raven Room restaurant. ✗ RAVEN ROOM

⓫ Sitka's centerpiece is **St. Michael's Russian Orthodox Cathedral**, its green-painted onion dome and conical cupola visible from all over town. Its cornerstone was laid in 1844 and the original cathedral consecrated by Bishop Innocent on November 20, 1848. The present-day building is an exact replica of the original, which burned on January 2,

## "PARIS OF THE PACIFIC"

During the 1800s, Sitka was the largest city on the west coast of North America. It became known as the "Paris of the Pacific" for its commercial, social, and cultural activities. Ships of many nations called there. Furs were the main export to European and Asian markets, but fish, lumber, and ice also were exported to Hawaii, Mexico, and California. (Ice from shallow Swan Lake—packed in sawdust from the local sawmill—sold in San Francisco in the 1850s for $7 a ton, less 20 percent for melting.) The Russian shipyard built and repaired vessels and their foundry produced the bells not only for Sitka's original St. Michael's Cathedral, but also for numerous Spanish missions along the Camino Real Trail in California.

1966, in a fire that destroyed the central business district. The night of the fire, as the building burned around them, heroic Sitkans risked their lives forming a human chain to hand the valuable treasures out of the building. Most moveable objects were saved, including the heavy entry doors and priceless icons—some dating to the fourteenth century. The original bronze bells, cast in Sitka's Russian foundry, were among the items lost.

Using the original blueprints, a new, fire-resistant cathedral was reconstructed over the next 10 years. New bells were cast from the melted remains of the originals and today all the rescued treasures are back in their original places. St. Michael's is an active church and the seat of the Russian Orthodox Church in Alaska.

Open daily, 7:30 a.m.–5:30 p.m. during the summer, unless otherwise posted. In the winter, open Mon.– Sat., 1:30–5:30 p.m. Other hours by appointment. $1 donation. Call (907) 747-8120.

🚶 *From the front door of the cathedral, walk to the left across Lincoln Street to the Lutheran Church.*

Near the cathedral are two banks with ATMs. 🏧

⓬ **Sitka Lutheran Church**, 224 Lincoln Street, is the third church on this site, which was never in the possession of the United States, being deeded directly to the congregation by the Russians. The first church, built in 1841–43, was torn down in 1888. In 1940, a new congregation built another church—which burned in the 1966 fire. The present church was built in 1967.

🏃 *Continue to the right (west) on Lincoln Street.*

The Ben Franklin Store at 216 Lincoln Street is noteworthy because this particular store is a direct descendant of the Russian-American Company, being owned by the Alaska Commercial Company, which formerly was the Northern Commercial Company, which in turn traced its roots back to the Russian company.

**13** At 202/206 Lincoln Street is "**Building 29**," one of only two Russian-American Company buildings remaining in Sitka. Building 29 was so-named because that was its number on the map drawn up to inventory Sitka's assets during the transfer from Russia. Building 29 was con-

structed in about 1835 to house employees of the Russian-American Company. Notice the "new" addition on the righthand side of the building, constructed in 1884. A National Historic Landmark, the building is considered the finest remaining example of Russian secular architecture in Alaska. The Backdoor Cafe is in the back of Old Harbor Books, across the way at 201 Lincoln Street. ✕ BACKDOOR CAFE

🏃 *From Building 29, cross Lincoln Street, turn right and continue past the cathedral to Cathedral Way. Turn left on Cathedral a block to Seward Street and turn left (west).*

**14** At Cathedral Way and Seward Street is **Rose Hill Place** (315 Seward Street). Now a shop, this Colonial Revival-style house was built in 1911 as the home of Miss Mae Mills, sister of early-day Sitka merchant

*Above:* Faithful to the original, some of the windows in St. Michael's Cathedral are painted. Glass was costly in Russian times; fakes gave the impression of more windows.

*Above:* Magnificent icons can be seen at the cathedral and the Chapel of the Annunciation in the Bishop's House.

and banker W.P. Mills. Miss Mills used her large house as a home for orphans. She planted the large Balm of Giliad tree in the front yard.

🚶 *Continue west on Seward Street one block to Observatory Street.*

⓯ On the hill at Seward and Observatory Streets is a large white house with a gambrel roof. Now known as the **Forest Service House**, it was built in 1916 by the U.S. Department of Commerce, Coast & Geodetic Survey, as offices and living quarters for the staff in charge of the seismological and geomagnetic observatory. It now houses Tongass National Forest personnel. Prior to 1867, this was the site of the Russian Tea Garden.

🚶 *Continue west on Seward Street for a few blocks to Marine Street, passing American, Princess, and Barracks Streets.*

---

OPTION: Turn up Princess Street for half a block. To the left is the grave of **Princess Adelaide Ivanovna Maksoutoff**, who died in 1862. She was the first wife of Prince Dimitrii Maksoutoff, the last of the 14 Russian governors of Sitka. At the end of the street is the old Lutheran Cemetery.

🚶 *Return to Seward Street and turn right.*

---

⓰ At the end of Seward Street is the **Russian Blockhouse**. Just above the blockhouse is the old **Russian Orthodox cemetery**.

The blockhouse is a replica of those that stood along a Russian stockade built after the Battle of Alaska in 1804. The stockade was torn down in

1877 and the original blockhouses razed in the early 1900s. The replica was built by the U.S. Park Service in 1958; it is not open to the public. There are good views of Sitka Sound and O'Connell Bridge from the blockhouse.

🕺 *From the left side of the blockhouse, follow the path and steps down the hill to Katlian Street and turn left.*

OPTION: Once you reach Katlian, turn to the right and walk about a block.

On the lefthand side of the street is the **Alaska Native Brotherhood Hall**. A Registered Historic Landmark, the ANB Hall was built in 1914 for the Alaska Native Brotherhood, founded in Sitka in 1912 to fight discrimination against Alaska Natives. Today, the ANB and the Alaska Native Sisterhood remain influential in preserving Native culture.

🕺 *Retrace your steps to the Pioneers' Home.*

**17** The **Pioneers' Home** dominates the western waterfront. Its grounds are on the site of the old Russian parade ground. When the first Territorial Legislature convened in 1913, it first gave women the right to vote, then established this Pioneers' Home as a haven for aging prospectors. Today there are several such homes around the state. This yellow stucco building with red tile roof was constructed in 1934; a women's wing  was added in 1956. The home has about 150 residents. Visitors are welcome. On the first floor, a gift shop sells handicrafts made by the residents.

The $13\frac{1}{2}$-foot-tall clay and bronze statue is "The Prospector." Sculptor Alonzo Victor Lewis used a real pioneer, William "Skagway Bill" Fonda,

*Left:* White picket fences surround graves in the old Russian Orthodox Cemetery near the blockhouse. *Above:* This replica of a Russian blockhouse was built by the U.S. Park Service in 1958. *Right:* A genuine pioneer miner posed for this bronze sculpture in front of the Pioneers' Home.

## HAPPY LANDINGS

Flying into Sitka can be a thrilling experience, especially if it's your first time. The 6,500-foot runway is about three-quarters surrounded by water, so it's like landing on a really large aircraft carrier. You always seem to find yourself wondering if the plane is going to stop before it runs out of pavement. (It does.)

Prior to the opening of the airport in 1967, and the O'Connell Bridge (the first cable-stayed, girder-span bridge in the United States) in 1972, Sitkans flew between their island city and Juneau aboard amphibious PBY Catalinas or float-equipped aircraft—and were ferried between downtown Sitka and Japonski Island via small shore boats.

as the model. Dedicated to the thousands of prospectors who pioneered Alaska, the statue was unveiled on Alaska Day, October 18, 1949.

The Pioneers' Home is a great place to see **Sitka roses**. They're all over town, but especially bountiful here. The hedge blooms through the summer; in late September you'll see red rose hips.

🚶 *From the Pioneers' Home, cross Katlian to Totem Square.*

**⓲** Katlian Street, bordering **Totem Square**, is on the site of the Russians' shipyard. Totem Square was filled in during 1940–41 as a WPA project. In addition to the central totem pole, there's a Russian cannon and three huge anchors believed to

have been lost from ships in Sitka Harbor in the 1700s.

On the north side of Totem Square (to the right as you face the water) is the Sitka Ranger District, Tongass National Forest (201 Katlian St., Suite 109). The very helpful staff dispenses information about trails, Forest Service cabins, campgrounds, and more. Open Mon.–Fri., 8 a.m.–5 p.m. Call (907) 747-6671 for information. A postal substation is in the same building as the Sitka Ranger District.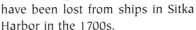

🚶 *From Totem Square, head south across Lincoln and turn right for half a block to the corner.*

You'll pass the former Post Office and U.S. Courthouse Building, which now houses the offices of the City & Borough of Sitka.

**⑲** Across the street, to the left, is the **Alascom Sitka Cable House**, built about 1904 for the Washington-Alaska Military Cable and Telegraph System (WAMCATS). WAMCATS was an overland and submarine cable telegraph system linking scattered  military posts in Alaska with the Lower 48. Built between 1900 and 1904, the cable operated until 1913, when a network of radio stations took over.

🚶 *Retrace your steps back up Lincoln. A sign points the way to Castle Hill on a path between the drugstore and the municipal building. Walk up the 78 steps.* 📷

**⑳** **Castle Hill**, a 60-foot-high rock outcropping, is the oldest state park in Alaska and a National Historic Landmark. Before the Russians arrived in 1799, the hill, known as Nu-Tling, was occupied by the four main houses of the Kiksadi Tlingits. Russian Governor Baranov built the first of four residences that stood on this hill during the Russian period. The last one, built in about 1837, was called Baranov's Castle (although he had long since departed Sitka). It burned in 1894.

Castle Hill is the site of the transfer of Alaska from Russia to the United States on October 18, 1867, as well as the site where the first 49-star American flag was raised on July 4, 1959, in honor of Alaska statehood. Around the perimeter are six Russian cannon, two bearing the double eagle insignia of Imperial Russia. A plaque depicts

Baranov's Castle at the time of the transfer.

The hill offers panoramic views of downtown Sitka, Sitka Sound, cruise ships, and the O'Connell Bridge, a 1,225-foot span linking Sitka and Japonski Island, site of the airport. Across the sound on Rockwell Island is a white-and-red "lighthouse," possibly the most-photographed home in Sitka. Not an official lighthouse, the private residence and inn was built in 1985. 📷

🚶 *Descend Castle Hill via the trail down the side facing the sound. The trail splits at the bottom. To return to Lincoln Street, veer left through an alley. To continue the walking tour, turn right to Harbor Drive, then turn left. Cross Harbor Drive and continue left for about a block and a half to the library.*

On the way, you'll cross Maksoutoff Street. To the right, the street ends on a 400-foot causeway to a little island. At the very end, #1 Maksoutoff Street was built in 1915 on the foundation of a former Russian fish saltery by merchant and banker W.P. Mills.

**㉑ Kettleson Memorial Library**, 320 Harbor Drive, was dedicated on October 18, 1967, the centennial of the Russian transfer of Alaska. It was partially funded by and named for Theodore Kettleson, who managed the Pioneers' Home and co-founded the First Bank of Sitka.

The library has a collection of books about Alaska and Pacific Northwest Indians. Call (907) 747-8708 information. 📶 ♿

🚶 *From the library, walk back to Harbor Drive and turn right to return to Centennial Hall and the end of this walking tour.*

*Above:* St. Michael's Cathedral dominates the scene in downtown Sitka.

# Getting Out of Town

## TAKE A HIKE: GAVAN HILL TRAIL

This trail is easily accessible from downtown Sitka. Just walk east on Lincoln to Baranof Street and follow Baranof about eight blocks to the end. The trail head sign is just past the house at 508 Baranof Street.

It's 3 miles to the summit of Gavan Hill, but it'll take you 3 to 4 hours going up because of a fairly strenuous 2,500-foot elevation gain. The planked, stair-stepped trail provides good access to alpine country and offers excellent views of Sitka and its surrounding area. There's a hut at the summit for shelter.

## TAKE A HIKE: INDIAN RIVER TRAIL

The Indian River Trail also is easily accessible from downtown Sitka. Head north on any street—Lake, Monastery, Baranof, Jeff Davis—to Sawmill Creek Boulevard and turn right. Walk 10 to 15 minutes to the Indian River Road—it's unmarked, but it's the next road past the Alaska Public Safety Academy. If you drive, there's parking outside the gate. Follow this road about half a mile to its end at a pump house. The trail head sign is just west of the pump house.

This is an easy walk through the rain forest. (Remember, the operative word here is "rain," so be prepared for wet and muddy conditions.) The trail is 5.5 miles long, and the estimated one-way time to the waterfall at the end is 4 hours. The trail climbs very gradually, for an elevation gain of 700 feet.

This trail up a wide valley offers magnificent views of the surrounding mountains. There are numerous picnic spots. Bears may be present, particularly when salmon are spawning. But you may see other animals—maybe a deer—and birds.

## FOR THE BIRDS: ST. LAZARIA ISLAND

The breeding grounds for thousands of seabirds, 65-acre St. Lazaria Island National Wildlife Refuge is located about 15 miles from Sitka as the puffin flies. In addition to tufted puffins, visitors will see rhinoceros auklets, murres, ancient murrelets, storm petrels, cormorants, and numerous other birds, including bald eagles. The surrounding waters are home to humpback whales, sea otters, sea lions, and harbor seals. The volcanic island was designated a wildlife refuge in 1909 and became part of the Alaska Maritime National Wildlife Refuge in 1980.

The birds and wildlife are best viewed from a boat. It takes approximately 45 minutes to an hour to reach the island from Sitka, depending on weather and sea conditions (take precautions if you're prone to motion sickness). Several tour companies operate excursions to St. Lazaria, including Raven's Fire, (907) 747-5777; Harbor Mountain Charters, (907) 747-0546; and Sitka's Secrets, (907) 747-5089. For other tour options, check with the Centennial Building Visitors Information Desk, 330 Harbor Drive, (907) 747-3225.

### FOR THE BIRDS: STARRIGAVAN PLATFORM

The Starrigavan Bird Viewing Platform is located near the end of Halibut Point Road, just past the Alaska Marine Highway terminal.

A 500-foot boardwalk and interpretive trail provides access through forest and wetlands for viewing spawning salmon, as well as waterfowl including great blue heron, kingfishers, loons, scoters, harlequin ducks, and mergansers.

### A WHALE OF A GOOD TIME

Sitka has some of the best humpback whale watching in the world and the city's new Whale Park (dedicated in 1995) provides an opportunity to view them, as well as Steller sea lions and other marine mammals. They congregate in Sitka's waters in the early fall and winter to feed on herring.

Sculptures of cavorting whales greet you at the entrance to Whale Park, located on a cliff about 6 miles south of town on Sawmill Creek Road. There are also a sheltered picnic pavilion, viewing scopes, boardwalks and a stairway to the beach.

Whales also may be seen on marine wildlife tours available from several companies, including Sea Otter & Wildlife Quest, (907) 747-8100; Bare Island Charters, (907) 747-4900; or Expeditions North, (907) 747-4400. For other tour options, check with the Centennial Building Visitors Information Desk, 330 Harbor Drive, (907) 747-3225.

## ABOUT THE AUTHOR

Author Julianne Chase grew up in the Great Land, where she graduated from the University of Alaska, Fairbanks. She worked as a newspaper reporter and editor for over fourteen years, and has written and edited two other travel guides, *Alaska Wilderness Milepost* and *Backcountry Alaska*. Juli currently resides in Seattle, where her work with a major cruise line enables her to continue exploring the grand state to the north.